GOD
VIBRATIONS

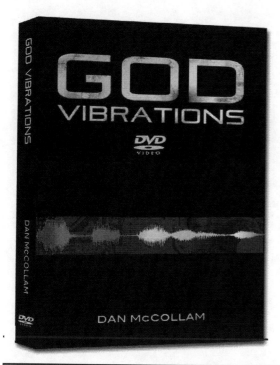

Though this study guide can certainly be read and enjoyed on its own, it was created as a companion to the DVD set *God Vibrations* in which these concepts are taught in a seminar setting. Each chapter includes fill-in-the-blank statements (answers are found in the Appendix) for following along with the video segments.

TEAR OUT AND COMPLETE THIS FORM TO ORDER A DVD SET. MAIL TO THE ADDRESS BELOW. The DVD set can also be ordered through ibethel.org/store or store.imissionchurch.com.

QTY	ITEM	UNIT PRICE	TOTAL
	God Vibrations DVD set	$ 59.00	
	God Vibrations Study Guide book	20.00	
	God Vibrations DVD set with book	69.00	
	Bulk pricing listed below.		

Subtotal	
Tax Included	0
Shipping (See schedule)	
BALANCE DUE	

Shipping within the US:

$1.50 per DVD set.
$1.50 per book.
Maximum shipping charge of $20.00.
Inquire by email for international shipping rates.

Bulk pricing on books:
20% discount on quantity of 10+.
30% discount on quantity of 30+.
Inquire by email for bookstore or school pricing.

531 Morningstar Way
Vacaville, CA 95687

regina@missionvacaville.org
The Mission Church 707-448-3124

GOD VIBRATIONS

A KINGDOM PERSPECTIVE ON THE POWER OF SOUND

STUDY GUIDE

DAN McCOLLAM

PUBLISHED BY:

iWAR (Institute of Arts Resources) and SOUNDS OF THE NATIONS
6391 Leisure Town Road, Vacaville, California 95687

COVER DESIGN & PHOTOGRAPHY BY: Jared Teska
Teska Photography & Design
JaredTeskaPhotography.com

Printed in the United States of America

First Edition: July 2013

ISBN-13: 978-0985186340

ISBN-10: 0985186348

CONTENTS

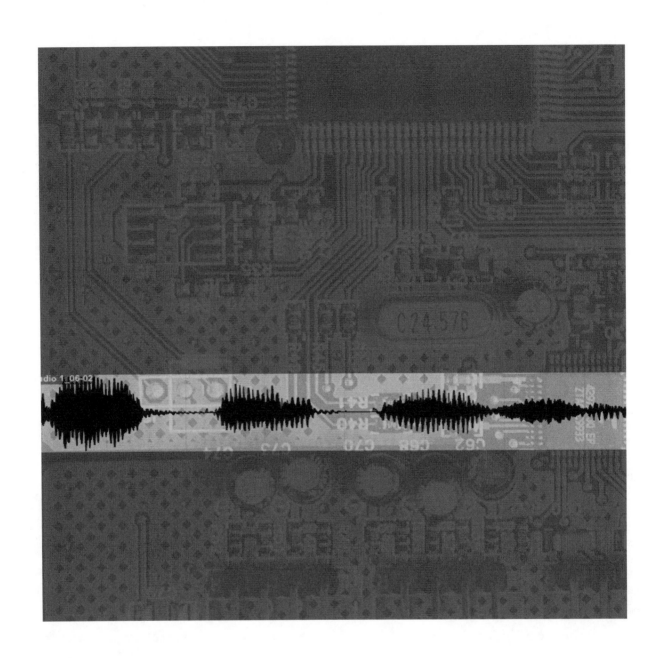

WHAT IF...

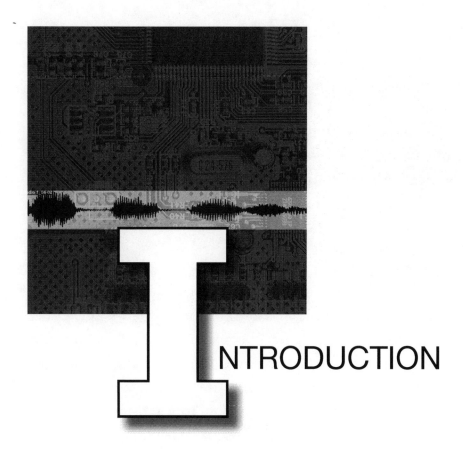

INTRODUCTION

Curiously, my personal journey into the power of sound did not originate in a university classroom or scientific laboratory, but rather, while guest-speaking in a primitive Bible school perched on a sandy hilltop in the South Pacific islands. Picture with me a beautiful tropical setting in which nestled a Bible training center filled with future spiritual leaders from five different island nations. These colorfully-clad young ladies and giant-sized men, clothed in their traditional wrap-around manskirts and sandals along with western button-up shirts and neck ties, stood in the sweltering heat of a tropical paradise passionately lifting their songs of praise to God. When the song leader broke into the old American hymn, "When The Roll Is Called Up Yonder," it first struck me simply as an odd song choice. I chuckled inside watching this native crowd singing western lyrics that were totally foreign to their language, culture, and understanding.

Hearing the hymn took me back decades to the very first time I heard it sung in a little country church on the fertile plains of Iowa. Even back in my youth, the hymn seemed old and out of place to me. As a teenager, the definitions of the phrases "the roll" and "up yonder" had to be explained to me, and I was pretty sure our island hosts were equally ignorant of the meaning of the Christian verbiage they were singing.

Suddenly my laughter turned to sadness as a question shook my spirit. "Where are the songs and the sounds of *this* nation?" I wondered. During this long worship service, the group of native worshipers had not sung one song that reflected the sounds, instruments, or musical style of their own nation. The injustice of it grew in my spirit like a mounting ocean wave. Other nations I had been to and people groups I had been with flashed through my memory—each group struggling through translated western songs in remote global settings—East Indians in a primitive village singing Darlene Zschech's "Shout to the Lord," gypsies in a shack near a Romanian railway lifting a chorus of Darrell Evans' "Trading My Sorrows," tribal Africans in the bush reciting the latest Chris Tomlin or Matt Redman song. There is, of course, nothing wrong with these amazing songs of praise. However, each of these native people had in some way been robbed of the beauty of their own unique culture and tribal sounds in the name of religion. Most of them were convinced their native sounds were evil.

I thought back to my own journey in authentic ethnic expressions of worship. The 1960s and 1970s were a time when the validity of modern music as a worship expression was hotly challenged in the church. Drums were considered "of the devil" because they sounded like African beats calling forth the spirits of false gods. Drums also represented timing, and some reasoned that there was no need for time in Heaven. A well-known author and Bible teacher claimed that contemporary music could curve your spine. Others reasoned that distortion on a guitar amp could not possibly be of God since its purpose was to "distort" a sound. My teen worship band was thrown out of many churches, coffee houses, and Christian venues for having a sound that expressed our own cultural preference. Though I never entered the battle of defending a certain style of music, I always felt that to worship "in spirit and in truth" must include the uniqueness of one's own musical tastes.

Later in life, a college class on music appreciation revealed that throughout church history different styles and sounds had come under attack. Singing in harmony was banned from the church for decades along with the "devil's play thing," better known today as the church organ. Yet, all of these ideas stood in stark contrast to the picture that Scripture gives us around the throne room of God with every tribe, and nation, and tongue worshipping the Lord.[1] God would not have made the distinction of tribes, nations, and tongues if the beauty and treasure of their ethnicity did not have significance to Him.

This revelation broke over me like a tidal wave. God loves variety. God loves flavors of worship as surely as Americans love dinner choices of Chinese, Italian, Mexican, and Indian. God craves the flavors of Earth's ethnicity in praise and worship. Our ethnic diversity is not the product of some form of social Darwinism with various features evolved to suit our ecological surroundings. Our musical differences reflect the aesthetic brilliance of a master builder, an unrivaled artist, and the consummate composer. God's universe is not merely functional; it is musical. God, as Creator, expressed extravagant and indulgent variety in His own creativity. For instance, He did not create just one type of flower, or fish, or bird, or tree. Rather, God indulged His creative genius in the formation of nearly endless variety and variation of form, color, and species within our universe.

God's creative nature stood in stark contrast to the worship that I had seen all over the world. Most of the countries I have been to have abandoned their own sounds, styles, and instruments in the context of praise and worship. In that moment, God called me on a mission to restore the ethnic sounds of the nations in praise and worship to the one true God. My heart began to beat with the firm revelation that God created the variety of all things and all people for His own pleasure.

As the huge ramifications of this call nearly swept me away, another question whispered in my spirit, "Could this be something more than just God's pleasure?" Certainly this mission was worth accomplishing if only for

---

[1] Revelation 5:9.

the pleasure of the Father, but new questions haunted me. "What if these ethnic sounds have further power or significance in the universe? What if, beyond the pleasure of God, some greater purpose might be accomplished in releasing these sounds and frequencies for the glory of God?" With these types of questions, my quest into the power of sound began.

I began to pour through the Bible for answers to my new questions. In addition to the Bible, I also read books on quantum physics and alternative medicine. It seemed that Christians had not previously written much on the power of sound, so my search cautiously extended to extra-biblical and even ancient sources. For many years, I studied and compiled thousands of pages of research. Though I'm not in any way a scientist, physicist, doctor, or homeopath, the Holy Spirit helped me to grasp the significance of many of these truths and make them simple for others to understand. Still, there are certainly concepts in this study that are beyond my ability to explain. I suggest that together we observe these theories and truths like spectators at the Grand Canyon, eyeing them with a sense of awe and wonder, both at their creative genius and their mighty potential for Earth-shaking applications. In the end, I believe that the study of the power of sound helps us know the importance of our conversations, our self-talk, our prayers, our declarations, and our praises.

Using the Study Guide

Though this study guide can certainly be read and enjoyed on its own, it was created as a companion to the DVD set *God Vibrations* in which I teach these concepts in a seminar setting. I have included in each chapter fill-in-the-blank statements, (answers are found in the Appendix), for following along with the video segments. If you don't have the video, you can still benefit from the research, but the experiments demonstrated in the video will help you visually grasp the power of sound on a whole new level. In this study guide you will find quotes extracted from my years of research. There are suggested experiments you can try in order to experience your own observations into the power of sound. "Questions for Group Discussion," (or personal reflection), are provided for each chapter along with a "Life Application" section. Finally, each of the six studies concludes with a short list of resources for further study and research.

You may also want to consider the sister book to this volume, *God Vibrations: A Kingdom Perspective on the Power of Sound*. While the book covers some of the same material as this study guide, it goes into more depth, and I believe you will appreciate its comprehensive exploration.

My personal study of the power of sound has changed how I view worship, prayer, and even simple conversations. My hope is that *God Vibrations: A Kingdom Perspective on the Power of Sound Study Guide* will be a blessing to you and everyone you share it with.

Let your journey begin.

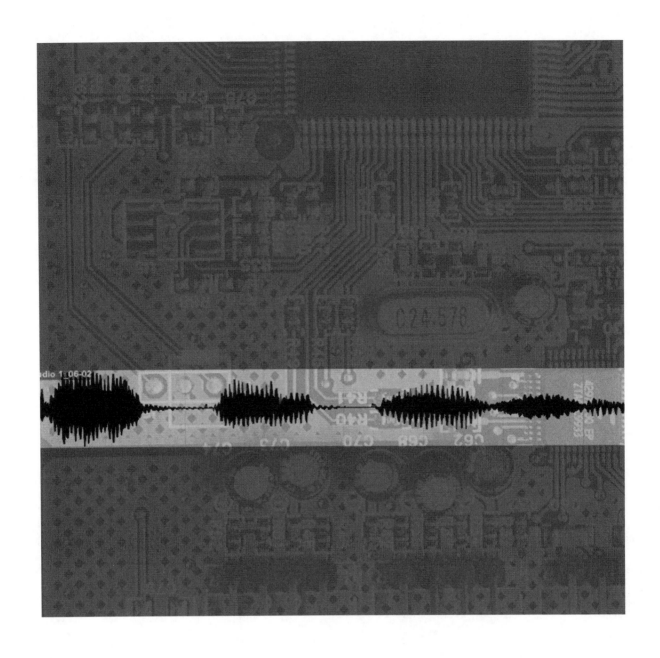

WHAT IF THE TINY VIBRATING STRAND OF ENERGY THAT SCIENCE CALLS "STRINGS" IS ACTUALLY GOD'S VOICE?

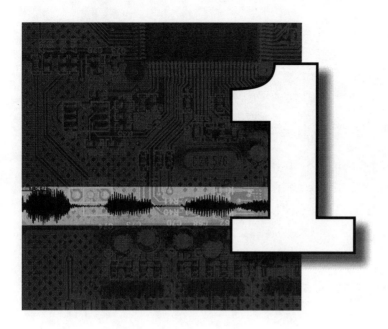

Frequency:
Everything Vibrates

Much of the research we will use in this study is from scientific or extra-biblical sources. Using these sources is not an endorsement of any of the belief systems, conclusions, or agendas of the original authors. In my research, I found it helpful to exercise spiritual discernment and avoid anything that troubled my own spirit. I give you full permission to do the same.

Sound Foundations

For this journey, I also felt like God gave me some boundaries or foundation stones for staying within the context of Scripture. The following Scriptures form the boundary lines for what I would consider sound foundations.

First Foundation Stone

Through him all things were made; without him nothing was made that has been made. (John 1:3)

1. Anything we introduce as truth today was made by _____. From John chapter one, we understand that God created all things and there is nothing that exists that He did not make.

2. The devil did not make _____; the devil is not a _____.

3. We do not want to do for the devil what he _____ _____ for himself. (See Isaiah 14:12-14 and Ezekiel 28:12-19. Many theologians believe these prophecies are a double reference to the kings of that day and to Lucifer before his fallen state.) God alone is the Creator, and we don't want to exalt anything above God or His throne by saying or implying that "the devil made that."

Second Foundation Stone

For by him all things were created in heaven and on earth, visible or invisible, whether thrones or powers or rulers or authorities; all things were created by him and for him. He is before all things, and in him all things hold together. (Colossians 1:16-17)

4. God didn't just make visible things; He also made the _____ things. Much of sound belongs to the invisible realm; but we clearly see that God created invisible forces and powers that could include the power of sound in the unseen realm.

5. The devil is still just a _____ _____ not a creator. This is demonstrated by the reference to thrones, dominions, principalities and powers in the invisible realm being created by God.

Third Foundation Stone

Thou art worthy, O Lord, to receive glory and honor and power: for thou hast created all things, and for thy pleasure they are and were created. (Revelation 4:11, KJV)

6. Everything in creation is still for the _____ of the Father. Many people believe that God originally created everything for His pleasure, but now, many things are too evil or corrupt to be redeemed. Revelation 4:11 demonstrates that all created things can still serve the pleasure, honor, and glory of God. There are truths out there about sound that belong to God, His Kingdom, and His children and we are here to redeem those things.[2]

7. One of the purposes of the Church in the world is to find things that have not been used for the honor, glory, and pleasure of God and _____ _____ back to their original purpose. We are not here to condemn; we are here to redeem, to restore, and to reconcile because of what Christ has done on the cross.

Vibration and Creation

8. If we want to understand the power of sound in our

---

[2] See Scriptures on the ministry of reconciliation: John 3:17-18, 2 Corinthians 5:18-21.

universe, we must simply remember that God used sound to _____ everything that exists. The Genesis account of creation explains that God spoke, and all things were created by the power of His voice.

Let's take a closer look at what happened in the beginning.

In the beginning God created the heavens and the earth. Now the earth was formless and empty, darkness was over the surface of the deep, and the Spirit of God was hovering over the waters. And God said, "Let there be light," and there was light. (Genesis 1:1-3)

Partnership of the Godhead in Creation

In the first three verses of the creation account, we see the partnership of all three persons of the Godhead in the act of creation.

Implications of Genesis 1:1

9. In the beginning, God the Father creates _____ out of _____. God the Father creates all the atomic particles that would be used for everything that is yet to be formed or shaped.

By faith we understand that the worlds were framed by the word of God, so that the things that are seen were not made of things that are visible. (Hebrews 11:3)

Renowned Christian scientist, Dr. Henry Morris, explains[3] that for matter to exist you need:

- ❖ nuclear forces
- ❖ gravitational forces
- ❖ electromagnetic forces

The Father created all the nuclear forces from the invisible realm that would be used to make the heavens and the Earth, but their structure is still described as "without form and void."[4] These atomic particles make up the nuclear forces—the physical structure or building blocks for all that would be created.

Significance of Genesis 1:2

The word "hovering" in Genesis 1:2 is the Hebrew word *rakhaf,* which, according to the Hebrew lexicon, means "to shake, flutter, or move."

> 10. Any of these terms refer to a rapid back and forth motion that in scientific terms could be called a
>
> _____.

Dr. Morris has a great explanation for these terms:

In modern scientific terminology, the best translation would probably be "vibrated...." Waves are typically rapid back and forth movements and they are normally produced by the vibratory motion of a wave generator of some kind. Energy cannot create itself.... If

---

[3] Source: Dr. Henry Morris, *The Genesis Record,* pgs. 56-57, Creation Life Publishers, San Diego, CA (1976).
[4] KJV.

the universe is to be energized, there must be an Energizer. If it is to be set in motion there must be a Prime Mover.... It is most appropriate that the first impartation of energy to the universe is described as the "vibrating" movement of the Spirit of God Himself.[5]

God the Father makes all the atomic particles. Then God the Holy Spirit energizes all the created matter with vibratory motions, such as gravity waves, sound, light, and other electromagnetic waves. The Holy Spirit generates the gravitational forces which allow physical matter to hold together—along with the sound waves—so that the voice of the Lord could be spoken over creation.

Psalm 104 reinforces the work of the Holy Spirit in creation.

> *When you send your Spirit, they are created, and you renew the face of the earth.* (Psalm 104:30)

Impact of Genesis 1:3

Jesus the Word then speaks: "Let there be..." and in so doing shapes the creation with the power of His voice. The voice is an example of vibrational forces—which shape and define matter.

> *In the beginning was the Word, and the Word was with God, and the Word was God. He was with God in the beginning. Through him all things were made; without him nothing was made that has been made.* (John 1:1-3)

> *By the word of the LORD were the heavens made, and their starry host by the breath of his mouth...For he spoke, and it came to be; he commanded, and it stood firm.* (Psalm 33:6, 9)

---

[5] Dr. Henry Morris, *The Genesis Record,* pgs. 56-57, Creation Life Publishers, San Diego, CA (1976).

For by him all things were created: things in heaven and on earth, visible and invisible, whether thrones or powers or rulers or authorities; all things were created by him and for him. He is before all things, and in him all things hold together. (Colossians 1:16-17)

11. Whatever Jesus the Word speaks, creation takes on the _____ of His voice.

This biblical account would suggest that vibrations, (gravitational and sound waves), are a key to the structure of all physical matter. One of the current theories of quantum physics states that the entire universe is in a continuous state of vibratory motion. In other words, modern scientific theories and the Bible agree that everything in the universe has a vibration at the center of it, or in simple terms, everything vibrates.

Vibration and String Theory

This concept, that everything vibrates, is similar to "string (or "superstring") theory" as described in the book and PBS Nova episode of the same title, *The Elegant Universe: Superstrings, Hidden Dimensions, and the Quest for the Ultimate Theory.*

Instead of a multitude of tiny particles, string theory proclaims that everything in the universe, all forces and all matter, is made of one single ingredient—tiny, vibrating strands of energy known as string....A string can wiggle in different ways, and the different ways in which the string wiggles represent the different kind of elementary particles....It's like a violin string, and it can vibrate just like a violin string can vibrate. Each note, if you like, describes a different particle.[6]

---

[6]   Brian Greene, *The Elegant Universe: Superstrings, Hidden Dimensions, and the Quest for the Ultimate Theory,* Vintage Books (February 29, 2000).

12. The sound wave that came out from the voice of Jesus Christ is what _____ everything that exists.

Could string theorists be proposing the same concepts as the Genesis account? Creation would suggest that God's voice, (or Word), is at the center of all creation. Could God's voice be the tiny vibrating strand of energy that science calls "strings"?

Vibration and Quantum Field Theory

A similar adaptation of theoretic physics comes from a unique application of quantum field theory. Simply put, this theory suggests that the quantum field in a scientific experiment is more significant than its manifestation, or, in other words, that cause is greater than effect.

> *This is the great mystery with sound, there is no solidity! A form that appears solid is actually created by an underlying vibration. In an attempt to explain the unity in this dualism between wave and form, physics developed the quantum field theory, in which the quantum field, or in our terminology, the vibration, is understood as the one true reality, and the particle or form, and the wave or motion, are only two polar manifestations of the one reality, vibration.* [7]

13. Quantum field theory would also suggest that _____ are what is holding all matter in the universe together.

Dr. Cathie E. Guzetta, author of several books and director of Holistic Nursing Consultants, offers her own application of quantum field theory to our physical universe.

---

[7] Beaulien, John: *Music and Sound in the Healing Arts,* Station Hill Press, 1987, p. 40.

The forms of snowflakes and faces of flowers may take on their shape because they are responding to some sound in nature. Likewise, it is possible that crystals, plants, and human beings may be, in some way, music that has taken on visible form.[8]

14. Jesus released the sound of His voice, and His voice caused things to take on _____, and form, and _____.

Isn't that similar to what Genesis chapter one is describing? God speaks and physical matter responds to the sound of His voice.

Sound Shaping Matter

For an example of how sound shapes visible matter, we can examine the experiments of Ernst Chladni, the father of acoustics. Consider the Genesis account and scientific experiments with the concept of sound shaping matter:

Many of the scientific concepts of sound shaping matter and the theories surrounding it are attributed to the man called the father of acoustics, Ernst Florenz Friedrich Chladni (1756-1827). In 1680, Robert Hooke of Oxford University drew a bow across a glass plate covered with flour and saw "nodal patterns" appear. Based on Hooke's finding, Chladni experimented with geometric shapes of thin glass or metal plates covered with fine sand sprinkled uniformly over the surface. By pulling a violin bow across these plates the vibration of the bow would cause complex geometric shapes to form in the sand. Chladni proved that the pressure derived from sound waves affects, (or shapes), physical matter.[9]

---

[8] Guzzetta, Cathie E.: *Music Therapy: Nursing the Music of the Soul, in Music: Physician for the Times to Come,* Campbell, Don (editor) Quest Books, 1991, p. 149.
[9] Chladni, Ernst Friedrich *Discoveries in the Theories of Sound,* 1787.

Chladni's physics experiment, also called a resonance square, is a great visual representation of what may have happened in the Genesis account of creation. Picture the evenly scattered particles of sand as the nuclear particles or atomic elements that God the Father created from the invisible realm. The vibration of the violin bow is like the moving of the Holy Spirit upon those particles to bring them to life. The sound wave itself is like the voice of Jesus the Word speaking specific form, shape, and detail into the yet formless universe. Of course, we believe that all members of the Godhead were involved in every aspect of creation, but there do seem to be some unique distinctions in their specific roles during the creative process.[10]

15. Through the resonance square we understand that sound has the power to shape _____ _____.

16. Prayer is not a wishing well; prayer is making the sound that _____ is making because creation still responds to the sound of His voice.

Fire Shaped by Sound

17. American Scientist, John Le Conte,[11] discovered that flames were sensitive to _____ waves.

Later work by other scientists showed that the height of a flame could be affected by transmitting sound in the gas supply. Heinrich Rubens used these discoveries in 1904 to create what is now called a "Rubens' Tube" by taking a 3-meter-long pipe and drilling 200 small holes into it at 2-centimeter intervals.

---

[10] The "God Vibrations DVD" illustrates the resonance square.

[11] American scientist, John Le Conte, was later named president of University of California, Berkeley 1858.

Rubens then filled the pipe with a flammable gas. After lighting the gas, all the flames rose to the same level; but when a sound was introduced to one end of the pipe, the flames would take on the shape of the standing wave or that specific sound wave.[12] The Rubens' Tube experiment is another example of sound's observable impact on the fundamental elements of creation.[13]

Understand that what we perceive as sound is actually just vibrating molecules. It isn't interpreted as sound until the cilia in our ears respond to the vibration. This is called air conduction.

Frequency

18. We are seeing that everything in the universe _____. Everything in the universe is in a continuous state of vibratory _____.

19. Frequency, as it relates to vibrations, is the scientific term referring to the measurement of the _____ at which matter vibrates. It's another way of asking, "How frequent are the cycles of that wavelength?"

The earth vibrates between 6-10 hertz. This means that the earth normally vibrates 6 to 10 times every second.

A human can detect sound as low as 20 hertz and as high as 20,000 Hz (20 khz), while some species of dogs can detect frequencies up to 60,000 hertz, or cycles per second. The highest note reproducible by the average female human voice is a sixth octave C that cycles at 1046.5 times per second.

---

[12] M.D. Gardner, K. L. Gee, G. Dix, *An Investigation of Rubens Flame Tube Resonances*, J. Acoustic Society Am. Volume 125, pp. 1285-1292 (2009).
[13] You will find the video clip of Rubens' Tube on the "God Vibrations DVD."

For further reference, the lowest note on a grand piano is the low C that cycles at 65.4 times per second. The highest note, high C at eight octaves higher, cycles at 4186 times per second.

Because all matter vibrates, we know that everything in the universe has a unique frequency.

Conclusion

All matter vibrates. The entire universe is in a continuous state of vibratory motion. I believe God's voice, (or God's Word), is at the center of that vibration. He is the "string" that is holding all things together. He is the quantum field that is shaping the form of all things. The study in this chapter helps us to see the truth of the Scripture that all things were created by Him and for Him, and that in Him alone, all things consist, hold together, and have their being.

Life Application

We can definitely see that sound impacts our physical universe. We know from Scripture that God's voice shaped all created things. What impact might God's voice currently have on our physical reality?

Hebrews 6:18 states that it is impossible for God to lie. I once thought this to be true only because of God's holy nature and righteous character. Now I see it is also true as a scientific principle. It is impossible for God to lie because even if what God says were not true a nanosecond ago, the moment God speaks it, all physical particles in the universe scramble to come into alignment with His voice.

All of creation is tuned to the frequency of God's voice. I believe that all matter continues to respond to the sound that created it.

Questions for Group Discussion

1. How does God's scientific inability to lie affect your personal faith in His promises?

_____

_____

_____

2. How does sound's effect on physical reality impact the quality and content of your own personal conversations?

_____

_____

_____

3. What was the most intriguing concept for you from this lesson?

_____

_____

_____

Questions to Ponder

Let's explore some questions surrounding the following passage on creation.

For by him all things were created: things in heaven and on earth, visible and invisible, whether thrones or powers or rulers or authorities; all things were created by him and for him. He is before all things, and in him all things hold together. (Colossians 1:16-17)

1. What is the significance of God creating both the "visible and invisible" realms?

_____

_____

_____

2. What is the significance of the phrase, "All things were created through Him and for Him?" (Compare this idea to Isaiah 43:21, Romans 11:36, and Revelation 4:11.)

_____

_____

_____

3. In what ways do "all things consist" through Him?[14]

---

[14] KJV.

(You might want to do a word study on the deeper meaning of "consist" or consult other Bible translations for a fuller understanding of this passage in light of this lesson.)

_____

_____

_____

Further Study and Observation

To see more interesting patterns formed by sound, try the following home experiment.

Frequency Visualization Experiment: Dancing Cornstarch

Mix one cup of regular cornstarch with half a cup of water to form a thick pasty mixture. Stir thoroughly. Lay a stereo subwoofer speaker on its back with the speaker cone facing up. Carefully cover your stereo's subwoofer with a loose sheet of plastic wrap to protect the speaker cone. Pour the cornstarch mixture on top of your speaker cone and play some heavy bass electronic or rap music through the speaker. You can also use a tone from a tone generator program at 120 hertz.

The cornstarch should create interesting shapes and dance along with the sound. (For video examples of this experiment, go online to Youtube.com and search "cornstarch." My favorite is entitled "Non-Newtonian Fluid on a Speaker Cone." I also like the short clip from the television series episode of "Big Bang Theory: Starch and Water.")

Further Study and Research

There are many more researchers who have done studies on how we can visualize sound waves and their impact on the physical world around us. Below are names in bold type that I recommend for further research.

Jules Antoine Lissajous (1822-1880) was a French scientist and mathematician who used sounds of different frequencies to vibrate mirrors. A beam of light would trace different patterns depending on the frequencies of the sounds. His experiments are similar to a modern day laser light show. Resulting shapes are called "**Lissajous Figures**" and are still in use today.

Cymatics, the study of wave phenomena, is a science pioneered by Swiss medical doctor and natural scientist, **Hans Jenny** (1904-1972). For 14 years, he conducted experiments animating inert powders, pastes, and liquids into life-like flowing forms that mirrored patterns found throughout nature, art, and architecture.

Although his research cannot be documented as valid or actual science, you still may want to explore the theories of **Masaru Emoto** (born 1943). Emoto is a Japanese author and entrepreneur who claims that human speech and thoughts directed at water droplets before they are frozen can determine whether their snowflake-like shape will be beautiful or ugly.[15]

A note of caution: A triple blind follow-up study published in the *Journal of Scientific Exploration* did not yield the same results as Emoto's research, therefore, this particular example may be considered more of an idea or theory than actual science.

---

[15] *Messages from Water* Volume 1 (June 1999), Hado Publishing. *The Hidden Messages in Water* (April 2004, English) Beyond Words Publishing.

Notes

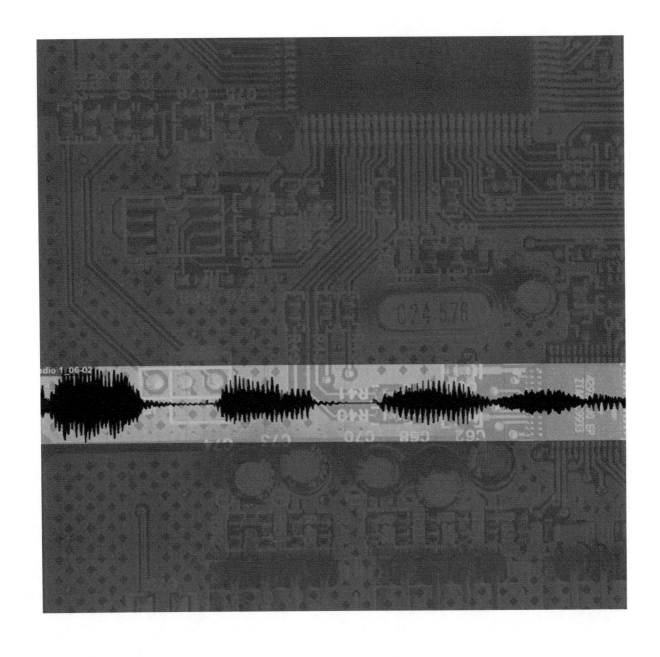

WHAT IF WE COULD HEAR
THE RESONANCE
OF THE
UNIVERSE'S VIBRATIONS?

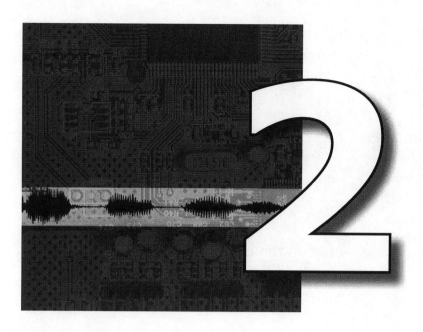

Resonance:
Every Vibration Makes a Sound

We know from the first chapter that the whole universe is vibrating. Everything vibrates. Additionally, scientists and researchers have determined that every vibration makes a sound (though not every sound can be detected by the human ear). While frequency refers to the measurement of the speed at which matter vibrates, resonance describes the prolongation of that vibration so that it can be heard or detected.

Resonance

1. Resonance literally means to _____.

The vibrations that are in a wine glass cannot be heard until the side of the glass is struck, causing it to resonate. When the glass is struck, the volume (decibels) of the wave increases and the vibration re-sounds so that its frequency can be heard. This is resonance.

      2. The entire universe is _____.

      3. All of creation is a _____ of sound.

What if we could hear the resonance of the universe's vibrations?

Data Sonification

Data sonification is a science invented for just that purpose. It interprets complex streams of data into audible sounds.

      4. Data sonification uses non-speech audio to _____ information or perceptualize _____.

To understand the value of data sonification, try to imagine which one of the following assignments you would most likely choose:

❖ Analyze a massive document with numbers running from margin-to-margin and top-to-bottom on each of its one hundred pages.

❖ Analyze the same number of alphanumeric characters by listening to a four-minute musical score that interpreted the characters as musical notes. (Picture the average number of notes in an orchestral or symphony score.)

Most people would choose to analyze that data by listening to a four-minute musical score or song. That is the power of data sonification, and it has been used for everything from animal research to studying mountains, stars, planets, and human DNA sequences.

Mountains Singing

I found an interesting example of data sonification in an article from a BBC[16] News source on the study of volcanoes. The article read as follows:

The low frequency seismic rumblings of volcanoes are being transformed into delicate musical scores in an effort to predict when they will erupt. Researchers in Italy have already created a concerto from the underground movements of Mount Etna in Sicily. By correlating the music with precise stages of volcanic activity from other volcanoes, the team hopes to learn the signature tune of an imminent eruption. 'If you can identify the musical patterns that warn of an eruption then you can implement civil protection measures days or even hours before the event,' said Professor Roberto Barbera of the University of Catania.[17]

    5. Before a volcano erupts it will sing a _____

_____.

When we consider the sonic research that is being done on mountains, I am stirred to ask the question, "Could it be that the multiple biblical references to mountains singing is something more than a poetic metaphor?"

*Sing, O heavens, for the L*ORD *has done it! Shout, you lower parts of the earth;* **break forth into singing, you mountains**, *O forest, and every tree in it! For the L*ORD *has redeemed Jacob, and glorified Himself in Israel.* (Isaiah 44:23, NKJV, emphasis mine)

Let the **mountains sing** *together for joy.* (Psalm 98:8, NASB, emphasis mine)

---

[16]   British Broadcasting Company.

[17]   Fildes, Jonathan, *Volcanic Eruptions Score Melodies,* BBC News, August 10, 2006.

If volcanoes sing a specific song before they erupt, do they sing other songs on happier occasions? Could these warning songs of the volcanoes be in any way related to the groaning of creation spoken of in Romans chapter eight?

For the anxious longing of the creation waits eagerly for the revealing of the sons of God. For the creation was subjected to futility, not willingly, but because of Him who subjected it, in hope that the creation itself also will be set free from its slavery to corruption into the freedom of the glory of the children of God. For we know that **the whole creation groans and suffers the pains of childbirth** *together until now.* (vs. 19-22, NASB, emphasis mine)

6. Creation is jealous for what man received in

_____.

7. Interestingly enough, creation is not waiting for the return of Jesus; it is waiting for the sons of God to

_____.

Singing Heavens

NASA has also performed data sonification of radio emissions emanating from stars and planets like Saturn, Jupiter, Earth, and the Sun and Moon.

8. Using plasma and wave instruments, the Cassini spacecraft, launched in 1997, began picking up sounds from Saturn while it was still _____ miles away.

9. The vibrational recordings are compressed and pitch-shifted down to put them in the _____ audible range.

One example of these recordings is the *Symphonies of the Planets*, a five-CD set released from NASA recordings that is now out of print. Put simply, it consisted of recordings made by Voyager 1 and Voyager 2 as they passed by the various planets and moons of our solar system. Although sound as we perceive it cannot travel in the vacuum of space, each planet and moon emits its own electromagnetic "signature" that can be picked up by the right instruments, and those emanations can be converted into sound that is audible and recognizable by human beings.[18]

The sound of planets, sun, moon, and stars are also spoken of in Bible texts.

> *Praise him, sun and moon, praise him, all you shining stars.* (Psalm 148:3)

> *The heavens declare the glory of God; and the firmament shows His handiwork. Day unto day **utters speech**, and night unto night reveals knowledge. **There is no speech or language where their voice is not heard**.* (Psalm 19:1-3, NKJV, emphasis mine)

Linear Transliterated Music

Written language can also be converted into music. Matthew Dahlitz, a composer and researcher from Australia, sent me orchestrated versions of the Hebrew language Bible text. On his website he explains the process.[19]

> *I have a matrix of scales and modes that match with the Hebrew alphabet. From the matrix I can "translate" the original text into musical tones. For example, if I take the C major scale, and assign the letter A to the note C, then the letter B to the note D, the letter C to the note E, and so on, I'll have a map to translate words into melody. Using this example then, the word "believe" would become*

---

[18] Samples of these recordings can be purchased online or downloaded from the NASA site. www.nasa.gov/mission_pages/cassini/.../pia07966.html

[19] Dahlitz, Matthew. *Linear Translation in A Nutshell.* http://matthewdahlitz.com

the musical melody D-G-G-C-G-C-G. We get repeated notes like the G because the letter "E" and "I" in "believe" happen to line up with G in the repeating 7-note scale when put up against our 26-letter English alphabet.

Of course, the matrix Matthew is using for the Scripture "transliteration" is much more complicated than this simple example. The main emphasis here is that language, words, and letters can also be expressed as music or encoded as sound.

Singing Cells and Proteins

DNA music has been in development since the early 1970s when geneticists found it easier to read the long strands of DNA code by assigning musical pitches to the 22 combinations of amino acids.

This allowed them to:

10. _____ DNA.

11. Look for _____ .

12. Reverse-engineer these _____ back into proteins.

The original study opened the way for musical scientists to develop the system further. Today DNA music is being taken seriously by composers.

In 2001, a genetic research company in California tried to use musical encoding to copyright DNA. If the proposal worked, it would mean that companies could, in effect, protect a particular DNA sequence against exploitation by competitors without the need for DNA patenting. Patenting DNA sequences has ethical questions attached to it and patent laws cover around 17 years in most countries. In contrast, song copyrights are free from ethical questions and can last 100 years or more.

"However, natural DNA sequences are generally considered **not to be covered by copyright as they are not original works of authorship.** They were not created by scientists, but simply uncovered," says Dr. Pam Stemmer, vice-president of research and development at Maxgen, a biotechnology company based in Redwood City, California. [20]

> *DNA music exists within every living organism universally, and now we have the technology to unlock a symphony from within everyone for a better and more aesthetic understanding of life, ourselves, and each other.*[21]

Perhaps this idea of a life song sheds new light on the death of Abel.

> *Cain told Abel his brother. And it came about when they were in the field, that Cain rose up against Abel his brother and killed him. Then the LORD said to Cain, "Where is Abel your brother?" And he said, "I do not know. Am I my brother's keeper?" He said, "What have you done?* **The voice of your brother's blood is crying to Me from the ground**.*"* (Genesis 4:8-10, NASB, emphasis mine)

As one Jewish rabbi described this verse, "Abel's song was absent in the halls of Heaven."

Conclusion

13. Every vibration makes a sound; it's called _____.

14. You not only have a _____; you are a _____.

---

[20] Conner, Steve, *The Independent Science,* Friday, March 22, 2002 (emphasis added within the quote). DNA copies may by protected as music.

[21] Stuart Mitchell (director, composer, producer of Yourdnasong.com).

No one else but you in all the world carries your song. If scientists can hear a vibration as sound, do you think that God can?

I believe that you are a unique song to the heart of God, and as such, possess a unique ability to touch and impact His heart.

Life Application

As a believer, you not only have a song of praise, you *are* a song. When you consider that every person on the planet has a unique DNA sequence, then you also understand that every person has a unique life song that no one else carries or has ever carried in all of history. I believe this fact speaks of our unique ability to touch the heart of God.

I like to compare it to favorite foods. There are many flavors in the earth that we enjoy and find satisfying, but when you are craving pasta, a steak just won't do.

Picture a stadium full of believers praising God. All of this is very satisfying and pleasing to the Father, but He is craving you. Your life is the only one that can generate that particular sound He desires. If a scientist can hear it, don't you think God can?

Let's review what we learned from this lesson on the death of Abel.

> *Now Cain said to his brother Abel, "Let's go out to the field." And while they were in the field, Cain attacked his brother Abel and killed him. Then the* LORD *said to Cain, "Where is your brother Abel?" "I don't know," he replied. "Am I my brother's keeper?" The* LORD *said, "What have you done? Listen!* **Your brother's blood cries out to me from the ground***.* (Genesis 4:8-10, emphasis mine)

If Abel's song was noticeably absent in the halls of Heaven, is your song's presence or absence also noted?

Take some time to meditate on the **sound of your life**. Remember your unique ability to delight the heart of the Father.

Questions for Group Discussion

One theory related to our lesson suggests that people are drawn to those who have similar musical patterns or intervals in their DNA sequence. The idea is that when we have similar sounding DNA, we can feel like we have known someone our entire life after just meeting them for a few minutes. Conversely, when we are turned off by someone whom we barely know, it is potentially because their life song is in dissonance with ours.

While this could explain some of our natural social tendencies, it does not excuse the command to pursue peace with everyone.

If it is possible, as far as it depends on you, live at peace with everyone. (Romans 12:18)

Turn from evil and do good; seek peace and pursue it. (Psalms 34:14)

1. Have you noticed a tendency to be drawn to certain people and repelled by others for no apparent reason?

_____

_____

_____

_____

_____

2. How do you seek and pursue peace with people that you are not specifically drawn too?

_____

_____

_____

_____

3. What is my Christian responsibility to people I don't personally "resonate" with?

_____

_____

_____

_____

Questions to Ponder

Paul's metaphor is descriptive of how believers are viewed by others.

You yourselves are our letter, written on our hearts, known and read by everybody. (2 Corinthians 3:2)

1. This is similar to the concept of you being a song. We have explored how our song impacts God, but what is the sound that **people** are hearing from your life?

_____

_____

Psalm 19 says that creation is speaking to us:

*The heavens declare the glory of God; and the firmament shows His handiwork. Day unto day **utters speech**, and night unto night reveals knowledge. **There is no speech or language where their voice is not heard**.* (Psalm 19:1-3, NKJV, emphasis mine)

Compare this to Romans chapter one.

*For since the creation of the world God's invisible qualities—his eternal power and divine nature—**have been clearly seen, being understood from what has been made**, so that men are without excuse.* (Romans 1:20, emphasis mine)

2. What is the sound—or voice—of creation saying to you about God?

_____

_____

Further Study and Observation

Resonance Experiment #1

Try this simple experiment. Step into your bathroom and close the door. Bathrooms with lots of tile are especially resonant. Now begin to hum the melody of a song that contains several varying notes. You should notice one note seems to sustain longer and sound louder than the others. This note is the dominant resonant frequency of your bathroom.

The room wants to naturally vibrate along with this particular note, and the note translates to the hard surfaces with less loss of energy and therefore seems louder. If you were to play an entire song in the bathroom with that root note as the dominant feature, then your bathroom would act as a natural amplifier for the vibrational structure of the song.

Resonance Experiment #2

If you have access to a hand drum like a conga, bongo, djembe, or darbuka, then hum a series of high to low notes into the open end of the drum. One note should cause the head of the drum to begin vibrating. When you hum that note's frequency, it will seem to echo or get louder and sustain longer. When you do, you will have found the dominant resonant frequency of that particular drum.

Transliteration Experiment

Use the following matrix to find a musical encoding for your first name. Circle the letters of your name to find the musical notes in the key of C that would represent the "sound of your name." Then play the musical notes on an instrument like a keyboard or synthesizer to find the musical transliteration of your name.

A B C D E F G H I J K L M N O P Q R S T U V W X Y Z
C D E F G A B C D E F G A B C D E F G A B C D E F G

Example: MARY

A B C D E F G H I J K L **M** N O P Q **R** S T U V W X **Y** Z
C D E F G A B C D E F G **A** B C D E **F** G A B C D E **F** G

The musical coding for the name "MARY" would be: A – C – F – F

Further Research on Data Sonification of DNA Songs

Compositions played for this lesson on the *God Vibrations DVD* were orchestrated by **Stuart Mitchell**. For more information, visit these websites:

www.stuart-mitchel.com   www.yourdnasong.com

Rosslyn Chapel is a fascinating study in the possibility of sound visualization being used in the architecture of this 15th century chapel. GOOGLE™ the "Rosslyn Chapel" for more information, and listen to samples of the music scores made from this research.

Notes

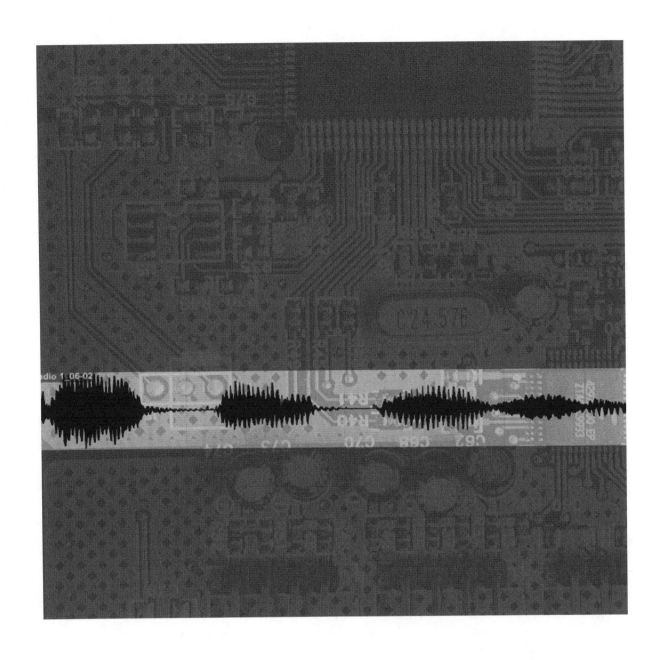

WHAT IF RESONANCE
AND ENTRAINMENT WERE
RESPONSIBLE FOR THE FALL OF THE
WALLS OF JERICHO?

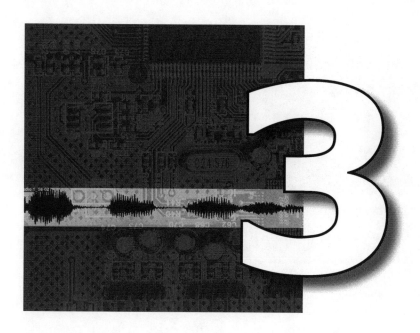

Entrainment:
The Breaker Power of Sound

We have learned so far in this study that everything vibrates and that every vibration makes a sound.

Entrainment

1. Entrainment is defined as the tendency of two oscillating bodies of the same frequency to lock into phase so that they vibrate in harmony or resonate

_____.

A scientist named Christian Huygens first discovered the principle of entrainment in 1665. While working on pendulum clocks, Huygens found that two identical clocks hung on a wall near one another would, by virtue of their similar frequencies, eventually swing their pendulums at the same rate, even if they started out of sync.

A Historic Bridge Collapse

*Broughton Suspension Bridge was a suspended-deck suspension bridge built in 1826 to span the River Irwell between Broughton and Pendelton, now in Greater Manchester, England. It was one of the first suspension bridges constructed in Europe. On 12 April 1831 the bridge collapsed, reportedly owing to a **mechanical resonance** induced by troops marching over the bridge in step. A bolt in one of the stay-chains snapped, causing the bridge to collapse at one end, throwing about forty of the men into the river. As a result of the incident, the* British Military *issued an order that troops should "break step" when crossing a bridge.*[22]

Breaking a Wine Glass

One the most common demonstrations of the power of entrainment is demonstrated in the breaking of a wine glass with the human voice. Enrico Caruso and Bengamino Gigli, Italian opera singers, are the first persons on record to have broken a wine glass using only the human voice.

The initial frequency of the wine glass is found by striking the side of the glass with your finger. The strike causes the crystal to resonate and a clear tone comes from the glass. If you match the pitch of your voice to the resonant frequency of the glass, the vibrating air will start the glass vibrating too. If you can do this with sufficient volume (usually 90–100 decibels) the glass will try to move in its vibration farther and faster than the material in the glass is able

---

[22] Wikipedia and Bishop, R.E.D. *Vibration* (Second ed.), 1979 (emphasis added in quote). Cambridge University Press, London.

to move, and the glass will break. What you witness in the glass breaking is called "resonant entrainment."

> 2. Through entrainment, vibrations can cause the structure of matter to become _____.

> 3. The same sound aimed at a glass will make it vibrate without even _____ the side or touching it at all.

Breaking Kidney Stones with Sound Waves

One medical treatment uses this same concept of resonant entrainment to break up something as tiny as a kidney stone. It's called ultrasonic lithotripsy.

> *Ultrasonic lithotripsy uses high frequency sound waves delivered through an electronic probe inserted into the ureter to break up the kidney stone. The fragments are passed by the patient or removed surgically.*[23]

It is not only the delicate crystals of a wine glass or the tiny calculi pebbles of a kidney stone that are subject to resonance. Resonance and entrainment have also been known to bring down huge architectural structures.

Collapse of the Tacoma Narrows Bridge

One of the most famous examples involving entrainment is the destruction of the Tacoma Narrows Bridge.[24] The bridge collapsed due to resonance, and other vibratory issues.

The first Tacoma Narrows Bridge opened to traffic on July 1, 1940.

---

[23] Kidney Stones Surgical Treatment, Kidney Stones, Urology Channel. www.urologychannel.com/Kidneystones/treatment-surg.shtml.

[24] Video footage of this bridge collapse is on the *God Vibrations DVD*.

Its main span collapsed into the Tacoma Narrows four months later on November 7, 1940, at 11:00 AM (Pacific time)...The bridge collapse had lasting effects on science and engineering. In many undergraduate physics texts, the event is presented as an example of elementary forced resonance with the wind providing an external periodic frequency that matched the natural structural frequency.[25]

Types of Sonic Weapons

VLF – Very Low Frequency Modulator

Modern scientists have harnessed the powers of resonance and entrainment for the development of "sonic weapons." During a 2009 G-20 summit in Pittsburgh, Pennsylvania, police used sound cannons to scatter protestors. Sonic weapons have also been used on cruise ships and other ocean vessels to ward off pirates. Though research on this subject can generate as many myths as facts, it does appear that sonic weapons can do all of the following:

❖ Focus a sound wave at a specific area from up to 1500 feet away.

❖ Cause a crowd to disperse because of physical discomfort.

❖ Injure or kill a person with extremely high decibel (volume) levels.

❖ Penetrate solid structures with sound waves.

LRAD – Long Range Acoustic Device

Long Range Acoustic Devices (LRAD) are neither myth nor legend. American Technologies Corporation has been producing them for military, maritime, and

---

[25] Billah, K,; R. Scalan (1991). *Resonance, Tacoma Narrows Bridge Failure, and UnderGraduate Physics Texbooks.* "American Journal of Physics," p. 59 (2): 118-124.

public safety use for over a decade. The device can focus a specific sound wave at a targeted location that can be as narrow as a single person or as broad as a crowd—so much so, that the Brooklyn Historical Society is currently using "hypersonic speakers" in a Vietnam veterans exhibit. When you stand in front of life-size photos of the veterans, the sound system automatically turns on and you hear the soldiers' pre-recorded stories. Many visitors can simultaneously experience the exhibit without hearing other sounds because the sound is so tightly localized, each patron hears only the intended sound.[26]

ULF – Ultra Low Frequency Weapons

These weapons claim that they can penetrate concrete buildings and potentially a moving motor vehicle. Emitting high-intensity infra-sounds can also impact humans in that they can disorient, reduce motor functions, and even stop a person's breathing.

Possible Biblical Examples of Sonic Warfare

We have seen the powerful force of sound break massive structures like bridges. Is it possible that this principle was utilized for the destruction of the walls of Jericho? We know that the Israelites were commanded to march around the city for six days without saying a word. Marching, as we know from the Broughton Suspension Bridge example, brings people into entrainment with one another and has the power to disturb large structures with resonance.

The Walls of Jericho

When the trumpets sounded, the people shouted, and at the sound of the trumpet, when the people gave a loud shout, the wall collapsed; so every man charged straight in, and they took the city.

---

[26] http://news.cnet.com.

(Joshua 6:20)

4. What happened as the Israelites marched? They were coming into entrainment with _____ _____.

5. From a spiritual dimension, that sound was the sound of _____ to achieve something that was impossible.

I believe that the Israelites were not allowed to speak so that they would not introduce other sounds or frequencies into the battle equation. The only sounds for three days were to be that of obedience and unity. On the seventh day, the troops were released to lift up a shout and a trumpet blast that brought down the walls.

6. The Israelites came into entrainment with one another and with the _____ of God, or Word of God.

Paul and Silas and the Prison Doors

Another potential example of spiritual sonic warfare occurred with Paul and Silas. After being severely beaten and chained up in the inner part of a prison, Paul and Silas disturbed the atmosphere with their prayers and praises. Evidently, Heaven began to resonate along, resulting in an earthquake that broke off every prisoner's chains and opened all of their prison doors.

And at midnight Paul and Silas prayed, and sang praises unto God: and the prisoners heard them. And suddenly there was a great earthquake, so that the foundations of the prison were shaken: and immediately all the doors were opened, and everyone's bands were loosed. (Acts 16:25-26)

This begs the question, "Are there sounds that God can release through us that have the power to break physical, spiritual, and emotional bonds off of others?" I believe there are.

7. When you make the sound that Heaven makes, you can _____ things off of people.

8. Your song, your prayer, your sound, your obedience can be the very thing that will open someone's _____ doors and break off their chains.

9. Why is there a destructive power to sound? Because Jesus came to _____ the works of the devil. (1 John 3:8)

Violence and Emotional Disturbance

Several urban legends speak of sound weapons that can cause a human being to become agitated, irritated, violent, and physically ill. While no research is currently available to prove or disprove these claims, we understand that sonic weapons can affect physical organs, bone structures, hearing mechanisms, and the intestinal track. Are these types of sonic influences possibly related to the dispersion and violence experienced in ancient biblical warfare?

Gideon

*And the three companies blew the trumpets and broke the pitchers, and held the lamps in their left hands, and the trumpets in their right hands to blow with: and they cried, "The sword of the Lord and of Gideon." And they stood every man in his place round about the camp: and all the host ran, and cried, and fled. And the three hundred blew the trumpets, and **the Lord set every man's sword against his fellow, even throughout all the host: and the host fled**....(Judges 7:20-22, KJV, emphasis mine)*

Jehoshaphat

And when they began to sing and to praise, the Lord *set ambushments against the children of Ammon, Moab, and mount Seir, which were come against Judah; and they were smitten.* **For the children of Ammon and Moab stood up against the inhabitants of mount Seir, utterly to slay and destroy them: and when they had made an end of the inhabitants of Seir, then everyone helped to destroy one another***.* (2 Chronicles 20:22-25, KJV, emphasis mine)

The operation of a long range acoustical device that produces a highly directional sound or the ability to broadcast sounds over a long distance is similar to some of the following biblical accounts.

Sound in the Trees

Do not go straight up, but circle around behind them and attack them in front of the balsam trees. **As soon as you hear the sound of marching in the tops of the balsam trees,** *move quickly, because that will mean the* Lord *has gone out in front of you to strike the Philistine army.* (2 Samuel 5:23-24, emphasis mine)

Lepers Feet

At dusk they got up and went to the camp of the Arameans. When they reached the edge of the camp, not a man was there, for **the** Lord **had caused the Arameans to hear the sound of chariots and horses and a great army***, so they said to one another, "Look, the king of Israel has hired the Hittite and Egyptian kings to attack us!" So they got up and fled in the dusk and abandoned their tents and their horses and donkeys. They left the camp as it was and ran for their lives.* (2 Kings 7:5-6, emphasis mine)

I am not in any way suggesting that those armies possessed or understood the power of sonic weapons. However, God certainly understands the principles and technologies behind these modern applications of science and weapons. The contextualization of modern sound weapons helps us better visualize and understand why these biblical armies responded the way they did.

> 10. What I want us to understand today is that the tongue is a _____ _____.
> Perhaps the most lethal sonic weapon in existence is the tongue.

> 11. We need to be careful what frequencies we are _____ ourselves with.

> 12. When we worship, when we pray, when we make prophetic declarations, we are not just begging; we are _____ with our physical universe.

We are interacting with scientific principles that God has put into play. He has put the power of life and death in our tongues.

> *The tongue has the power of life and death, and those who love it will eat its fruit.* (Proverbs 18:21)

> *A lying tongue hates those it hurts, and a flattering mouth works ruin.* (Proverbs 26:28)

> *The tongue also is a fire, a world of evil among the parts of the body. It corrupts the whole person, sets the whole course of his life on fire, and is itself set on fire by hell. All kinds of animals, birds, reptiles and creatures of the sea are being tamed and have been tamed by man, but no man can tame the tongue. It is a restless evil, full of deadly poison.* (James 3:6-8)

Conclusion

Sound carries the power to give life or to destroy. We need to be careful what frequencies we are aligning ourselves with. We must pray for a spirit of wisdom and revelation to align ourselves with what God is saying and doing.

Believers can use the power of sound and the tongue to create life, bring order and beauty, and to break off chains, open prison doors, and destroy the works of the devil.

Life Application

Entrainment can be demonstrated by watching children listen to music. Rarely will you need to ask a child to respond to music—they automatically start tapping their feet, dancing, or singing along. The entrained response to the beat and melody is almost automatic. Our bodies, mind, and spirit all desire to be in sync or harmony with the world around us.

I no longer see Proverbs 18:21 as a metaphor or some poetic device.

The tongue has the power of life and death...

I now believe that the tongue literally and scientifically embodies life-giving and destructive properties. When we understand the power of sound and entrainment to destroy, we are inclined to take the power of our words much more seriously.

Do not let any unwholesome talk come out of your mouths, but only what is helpful for building others up according to their needs, that it may benefit those who listen. (Ephesians 4:29)

The word "unwholesome" in the Greek lexicon is *sapros* which comes from the root *sapo* meaning "to corrupt or destroy." This definition emphasizes the fact that our tongue has destructive power. *Sapros* also means "rotten, putrefied, no longer fit for use, of poorest quality."

Yet, notice that our tongues can also build others up and literally benefit those who listen.

If you feel that you have been the target of the destructive power of words, then follow this simple pattern:

1. **Break any agreement with the lies spoken over you.** Don't come into "entrainment" or agreement with what has been said. If someone said, "You are stupid, ugly, or will never amount to anything," then take time

to break your personal agreement with that lie. Speak out loud, "I am intelligent. I am beautiful. I have purpose and a destiny." Counter the lies with the truth that God speaks and break the power of the sonic warfare or "word curses" against you.

2. **Forgive those who have spoken harsh words over you.** One of the reasons that unforgiveness is so destructive, is that when we refuse to forgive, we carry the weight of our sins and the heavy load of the other person's offense.

For if you forgive men when they sin against you, your heavenly Father will also forgive you. But if you do not forgive men their sins, your Father will not forgive your sins. (Matthew 6:14-15)

If you need help forgiving someone, then practice identification with Christ. When Jesus hung on the cross naked, abused, mocked, and beaten, He cried out words of forgiveness, understanding that the perpetrators did not know fully how their words and actions were affecting Him. Picture yourself hanging on the cross with Christ and calling out the same words to your own perpetrators.

Jesus said, "Father, forgive them, for they do not know what they are doing." (Luke 23:34)

Another point of identification that helps us forgive is to remember that God has first forgiven our offenses. Because we have all needed forgiveness and received it unconditionally from God, we can practice the same spirit of forgiveness over others.

Bear with each other and forgive whatever grievances you may have against one another. Forgive as the Lord forgave you. (Colossians 3:13)

3. **Speak blessings over the person who spoke the damaging words.** It is not enough to just forgive; we must return blessings where there were curses.

But I tell you who hear me: Love your enemies, do good to those who hate you, bless those who curse you, pray for those who mistreat you. (Luke 6:27-28)

Finally, all of you, live in harmony with one another; be sympathetic, love as brothers, be compassionate and humble. Do not repay evil with evil or insult with insult, but with blessing, because to this you were called so that you may inherit a blessing. For, "Whoever would love life and see good days must keep his tongue from evil and his lips from deceitful speech. He must turn from evil and do good; he must seek peace and pursue it." (1 Peter 3:8-11)

4. **Practice speaking the truth over yourself and coming into agreement (entrainment) with it**. Most people have unknowingly meditated on the negative things spoken over them; now it is time to meditate on the truth.

What does God say about you? God's words are the truest statements in the universe. What He says about you is not just a kind, patronizing compliment; it is the ultimate truth concerning you. Meditate on this truth. Speak it. Pray it as a declaration. Practice believing it. Express that truth in practical demonstration.

If you have been guilty of launching sonic warfare or harsh words against someone else, follow this procedure.

1. **Repent to the Lord** and confess what you have done.

If we confess our sins, he is faithful and just and will forgive us our sins and purify us from all unrighteousness. (1 John 1:9)

2. If the offended person is aware of your harmful words, **ask him or her for forgiveness**.

3. **Speak the truth** of God over them and bless them.

Questions for Group Discussion

1. How will your understanding of the literal power of life and death in the tongue affect the way you speak about yourself, others, and your situations?

_____

_____

_____

2. What does it mean to "live in harmony" with one another? (Romans 12:16, 1 Peter 3:8)

_____

_____

_____

3. How can we use our words (or sounds) to break things that need to be broken?

The Son of God appeared for this purpose, to destroy the works of the devil. (1 John 3:8b)

_____

_____

_____

Questions to Ponder

In our study we focused on the sonic warfare that Paul and Silas waged while they were stripped naked, beaten, and imprisoned. One of the goals of living victoriously is to learn to condition our responses to difficulties, troubles, trials, and persecutions. Read again the response of Paul and Silas to their unjust situation.

About midnight Paul and Silas were praying and singing hymns to God, and the other prisoners were listening to them. Suddenly there was such a violent earthquake that the foundations of the prison were shaken. At once all the prison doors flew open, and everybody's chains came loose. (Acts 16:25-26)

1. What is your usual response to trials, troubles, persecution, or an unjust situation?

_____

_____

_____

2. Have you ever taken joy into a difficult situation? Consider the following passages.

Consider it pure joy, my brothers, whenever you face trials of many kinds, because you know that the testing of your faith develops perseverance. Perseverance must finish its work so that you may be mature and complete, not lacking anything. (James 1:2-4)

Blessed are those who are persecuted because of righteousness, for theirs is the kingdom of heaven. Blessed are you when people insult you, persecute you and falsely say all kinds of evil against you because of me. Rejoice and be glad, because great is your reward in heaven, for in the same way they persecuted the prophets who were before you. (Matthew 5:10-12)

_____

_____

_____

3. How might changing your verbal response alter your own situation and break the warfare waged against you?

_____

_____

_____

Further Study and Observation

Resonant Entrainment Experiment

Take a crystal wine glass and place a straw inside. "Ting" the side of the glass with your finger or a spoon to hear the general pitch or frequency of the glass. Now place your lips 3-5 inches from the glass and sing the note you heard. If you match the frequency of the glass, the straw will start "dancing" or vibrating inside the glass. What you are seeing is an example of resonant entrainment. To actually break the glass you would need to sustain this note from 90-110 decibels until the glass vibrates and shatters. (We don't recommend trying this without the safety considerations of eye protection goggles and a safe area for broken glass.)

For further research on sonic weapons, search on the internet:

SARA Scientific Applications & Research Associates (maker of sonic weapons)

Future Weapons from Discovery Channel

LRAD Corporation

Sonic Cannons

Urban Funk Campaign

Freight Train Effect

Feraliminal Lycanthropizer

Vladimir Gavreau

More resources on the power of words or praise:

Power in Praise by Merlin R. Carothers

The Supernatural Power of a Transformed Mind by Bill Johnson

Power of Your Life Message by David Crone

The Supernatural Power of Forgiveness by Kris and Jason Vallotton

Notes

_____

_____

_____

_____

_____

_____

_____

_____

_____

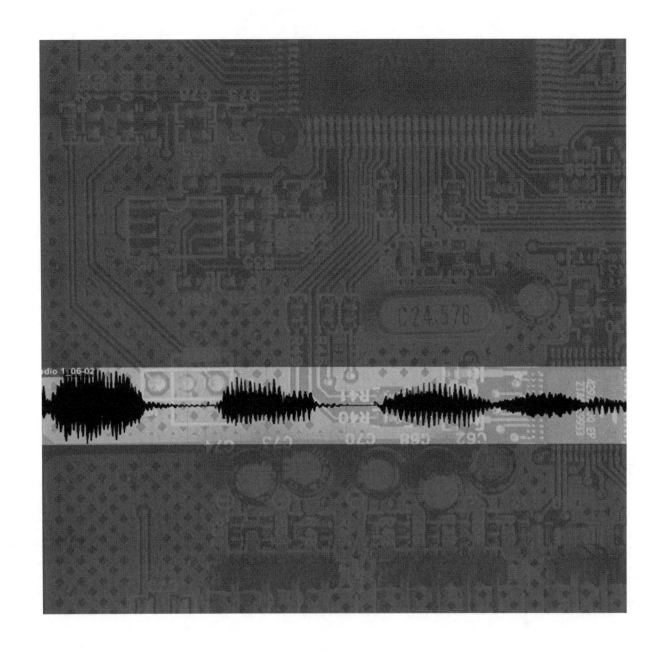

WHAT IF A
SONG COULD DRY UP
CANCER CELLS?

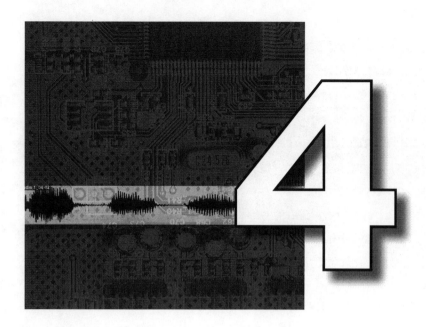

Harmony:
The Healing Power of Sound

We've seen the power of entrainment to break and destroy. Likewise, entrainment of sound, resonance, and harmony can have powerful positive impact.

    1. Frequencies can harmonize together in such a way that it releases _____.

The Rescuing Hug

A great example of the power of entrainment to heal occurred in October of 1995. Identical twin daughters, Kyrie and Brielle Jackson, were born premature at only two pounds each. Brielle was doing well, but nothing seemed to be working to stabilize the physical condition of her weaker sister.

Knowing that the one twin had little time to live, she put Brielle in the incubator with her sister Kyrie contrary to the hospital's rules. The healthier twin Brielle snuggled up next to Kyrie and put her arm over her sister in an endearing embrace. Almost immediately the smaller baby's heart rate stabilized and her temperature rose to normal. Her blood-oxygen levels, which had been frighteningly low, soared. She began to breathe more easily. The frantic crying stopped and her normal pinkish color quickly returned. Over the next weeks, her health steadily improved...The children survived their rocky beginning, and in time went home with their parents.[27]

Similar to the two pendulum clocks that Christian Huygens observed to discover entrainment, identical twins are the only human beings on Earth to share a common DNA code. Their core frequencies would be an exact match. In the same way that the two pendulums, formerly out of sync, began to sway together, the girls' heart rates, breathing rates, and blood pressures locked into phase. The dominant, or louder, of any two oscillating bodies on the same frequency will always influence the weaker.

In a spiritual and scientific sense, God's voice is always the dominant frequency in the universe because His is the voice that shaped all things.

Another method used to stabilize preemies is 'Kangaroo Care,' a term for prolonged skin-to-skin contact with parents and other caregivers...Proponents say the method can have amazing effects: a steadier heart rate, better breathing, greater contentment, deeper sleep.[28]

Cancer Cells Disrupted With a Song

In 1974, Fabien Maman, a French composer and bioenergeticist, explored the influence of sound waves on human cells. Together with Helen Grimal, a

---

[27]   Articles from *Life Magazine* and *Reader's Digest*, November 1995.

[28]   Article from *52 Best. Inc.*, 1999, "The Friday Morning Story." www.52best.com/hug.asp.

biologist at the French National Center for Scientific Research in Paris, the pair began a year-and-a-half study. Mounting a camera on a microscope, they photographed slides of human uterine cancer cells. Trying different instruments at low volumes (only 30-40 decibels), they searched for the most powerful instrument for impacting cancer cells. The duo discovered that the vibrations of the human voice are more powerful than any musical instrument.

> 2. According to Maman's research, the most powerful
> sound or instrument for affecting cancer cells was the
>
> _____ _____.

As Maman sang a nine-note musical scale into the diseased cells, a total explosion of the cancer cells occurred within just nine minutes.

It appeared that the cancer cells were not able to support a progressive accumulation of vibratory frequencies and were destroyed.[29]

Maman continued his study with two breast cancer patient volunteers. Each woman sang the nine notes for twenty minutes a day. The first woman's tumors totally vanished; the second woman followed through with a surgery where the doctor reported that the tumor had literally dried up.

Though it is not known whether a song or certain scale can heal or solve every situation, we are beginning to see the powerful impact.

Singing the Ten Commandments

The marriage between music and medicine is not a new idea nor is it a New Age idea. Professor Amnon Shiloah, former head of musicology at Hebrew University in Jerusalem, is considered a foremost authority on music in ancient cultures. The professor has published hundreds of articles on musicology and ethnomusicology worldwide and is credited with over one thousand entries in encyclopedias and research texts.

---

[29] Maman, Fabien (1997), *The Role of Music in the Twenty-First Century*, Redondo Beach, CA.

Shiloah speaks to the ancient connection between music and medicine.

Music, however, is found in every global context: history, geography, chemistry, mathematics, astronomy. Music molds the intellect, and medical texts have also employed it. You can read [in ancient texts] about how doctors should use music in treating a patient and when he should call in a musical expert to assist him...The Ten Commandments used to be sung, each in a different scale...so too were the chapters of Psalms, with each psalm having its own set of tones. The scales were also used for music therapy, a different scale for every illness...[30]

If this is all sounding a bit over-stated or contrived, it is helpful to remember that music therapy is an accepted and prescribed practice of the American Medical Association.

3. Music therapy uses music and all of its facets— physical, emotional, mental, social, aesthetic, and spiritual—to help clients _____ or _____ health.

Harps for Healing

Harps are not only an ancient prescription. MSNBC published a report in January 2006 on how harps are being used during open-heart surgery at Carle Heart Center in Urbana, Illinois.

Abraham Kocheril, chief of cardiac electrophysiology at the Carle Heart Center in Urbana, says he has found signs that harp music might help sick hearts...beat more normally...Some enthusiasts believe the harp has special healing qualities and Kocheril said resonant vibrations from live harp music may be particularly effective at regulating quivering heart rhythms. Other musical

---

[30] Ben Ze'ev, Noam. "Singing the Ten Commandments," December 12, 2005, www.haaretz.com.

instruments and recorded music might offer similar benefits... making a 'musical prescription' easier to follow.

Psychologist and harpist Sarajane Williams uses the instrument to help patients deal with chronic pain from arthritis, fibromyalgia, and other conditions. Patients at her Macungie, Pennsylvania, office sit in a reclining chair embedded with speakers that allow amplified vibrations from her harp playing to reach deep into aching tissue like a 'musical massage,' Williams said. She says the vibrations help relieve pain by stimulating circulation and relaxing patients.[31]

Dr. Mark Tramo is a neurologist at Massachusetts General Hospital and director of Harvard's Institute of Music and Brain Science. Tramo says that there is nothing "kooky" about the idea of entrainment and using music in healing. We already know that rhythmic music, for instance, can affect heart rates and rhythms, but more research is needed.

It is interesting in the biblical account that when the first king of Israel was suffering from the effects of an evil spirit, his cabinet members recommended calling a harpist.

Let our lord command his servants here to search for someone who can play the harp. He will play when the evil spirit from God comes upon you, and you will feel better. (1 Samuel 16:16)

Whenever the spirit from God came upon Saul, David would take his harp and play. Then relief would come to Saul; he would feel better, and the evil spirit would leave him. (vs. 23)

The results of David's instrumental music were three-fold:

---

[31] Associated Press, December 26, 2005: "Harp Can Soothe but Can it Heal?" and ccnworldnews.com.

4. Relief would come—that's _____ healing.

5. Saul would feel better—that's _____ healing.

6. The evil spirit would depart—that's _____ healing.

Music is one of the few things that affect humans on every level of consciousness.

7. Our psalms, our hymns, our spiritual songs are not just about God; they are actually designed to _____ and _____ one another.

Theories of Entrainment Healing

Theories of entrainment healing go back thousands of years and yet are newly being explored today. On a trip to the United Kingdom, I heard a well-known Bible teacher say that the opposite of sickness is not healing, but rather, harmony. When an organ or part of the body is vibrating out of tune or non-harmoniously, it is called "dis-ease" or disease. A body is in a healthy state of being when each cell and each organ creates a resonance that is in harmony with the whole being.

8. The opposite of disease is not healing; the opposite of disease is _____.

9. The theory of entrainment healing is that a body is in a healthy state of being when each cell, each organ, creates a _____ that is in harmony with the whole being.

10. The idea of entrainment healing is that when someone

is sick, they are out of _____, out of sync, out of resonance.

The Theory of a Healing Scale

The ancient people populating India had a scale they believed related to the frequency of body organs and specific musical notes. Though the ancients did not call these organs by their modern medical names, they did believe that specific areas and body functions were affected by specific notes and frequencies.

The following table of these beliefs is meant for informational purposes only and is not intended as an endorsement of this theory.

C	D	E	F	G	A	B
Blood	Pelvis	Stomach	Heart	Neck	Ears	Skin
Bones	Lower Back	Colon	Lungs	Mouth	Eyes	Muscles
Feet	Bladder	Kidneys	Back	Thyroid	Nose	Energy
Legs	Hips	Pancreas	Shoulders	Esophagus	Brain	Feelings

11. There is a dominant frequency over your whole _____ and over the distinct _____ of your body, and sound has the potential of either aligning or pulling out of alignment those particular frequencies.

Sound and our Bones

12. We not only hear with our ears; we also hear with our _____.

13. Hearing with our ears is called _____ conduction.

Spoken word vibrations may also be a key to healthy living. We learn from Dr. Alfred Tomatis that we human beings hear with our bones (bone conduction) not just with our ears (air conduction). Your skeletal structure vibrates with every word you speak. It may also vibrate or resonate with words and sounds that others make. The book of Proverbs seems to connect health of the bones, organs, joints, and marrow to words spoken over us. Consider the following passages for example:

- ❖ "Envy rots the bones...." (Proverbs 14:30)

- ❖ "A cheerful heart is good medicine, but a crushed spirit dries up the bones." (Proverbs 17:22)

- ❖ "The words of a talebearer are as wounds, and they go into the innermost parts of the belly." (Proverbs 18:8, KJV)

- ❖ "Good news gives health to the bones." (Proverbs 15:30)

- ❖ "Pleasant words are a honeycomb, sweet to the soul and healing to the bones." (Proverbs 16:24)

14. Our bones actually _____ with every word that we speak and with every word that is spoken over us.

15. Harsh words have the strongest negative impact over the body when they are spoken by someone you are already in _____ with.

16. When we re-align someone with the truth of what God is saying over them, then they experience _____ within their body.

The Healing Words of Jesus

He sent His word and healed them, and delivered them from their destructions. (Psalm 107:20, NKJV, emphasis mine)

17. There is something about the word of the Lord; there is something about the voice of the Lord; there is something about coming in agreement with the _____ that can release healing in a body.

But the centurion said, "Lord, I am not worthy for You to come under my roof, but just **say the word, and my servant will be healed**...*" And Jesus said to the centurion, "Go; it shall be done for you as you have believed."* **And the servant was healed that very moment**. (Matthew 8:8,13, NASB, emphasis mine)

When evening came, they brought to Him many who were demon-possessed; and **He cast out the spirits with a word, and healed all who were ill**. *This was to fulfill what was spoken through Isaiah the prophet:* **"He himself took our infirmities and carried away our diseases."** (Matthew 8:16-17, NASB, emphasis mine)

Conclusion

Based on Scripture, science, and medical research, it seems that there is a basis for belief that sound, music, and our words are connected to healing.

Life Application

The danger of sharing the scientific theories and the testimonies contained in this lesson lies in the temptation to follow forms and formulas rather than to be led by the Spirit. One could take the "healing scale theory" and try to sing or play A440 over every person with ear or eye trouble. We could try to find one scale that always bursts cancer cells like the research of Fabien Maman. The greatest key to healing resides in relationship with Jehovah Rapha—the Lord [Who] Heals.

The account in Acts 19 gives a healthy warning to those who would only want to follow formulas for healing.

God did extraordinary miracles through Paul, so that even handkerchiefs and aprons that had touched him were taken to the sick, and their illnesses were cured and the evil spirits left them. Some Jews who went around driving out evil spirits tried to invoke the name of the Lord Jesus over those who were demon-possessed. They would say, "In the name of Jesus, whom Paul preaches, I command you to come out."

Seven sons of Sceva, a Jewish chief priest, were doing this. One day the evil spirit answered them, "Jesus I know, and I know about Paul, but who are you?" Then the man who had the evil spirit jumped on them and overpowered them all. He gave them such a beating that they ran out of the house naked and bleeding.

When this became known to the Jews and Greeks living in Ephesus, they were all seized with fear, and the name of the Lord Jesus was held in high honor. (Acts 19:11-17)

There may be tendencies or keys that often release healing virtue that we can learn as students of the Word, of science or medicine, and as students of the Spirit. Our caution here is remembering that God created all things for His glory, honor, and praise. We do not want to exchange methods, principles, or formulas for the glory of God. Any healing method that truly works must be connected to the God Vibration that set all things in motion and holds all things together. Our goal then is to stay in relationship with Father, Son, and Holy Spirit to release His healing purposes in the earth.

Paul gives his spiritual son, Timothy, this same kind of caution.

> *But mark this: There will be terrible times in the last days. People will be...having a form of godliness but denying its power. Have nothing to do with them.* (2 Timothy 3:1, 5)

Make a commitment in your heart to the priority of relationship with God. Don't exchange true principles for the Person who is the Way, the Truth, and the Life. Let all things be done for the glory, honor, and praise of God.

Questions for Group Discussion

1. Have you ever seen a healing that was related to a song, a sound, or someone's words? Share your experiences with the group.

_____

_____

_____

2. Have you personally found any methods, formulas, or keys in healing that seem to have a high success rate?

_____

_____

_____

3. How do we keep these discoveries relational? That is, how can we distinguish between healing formulas or principles that work and the leading of the Holy Spirit in all things?

_____

_____

_____

Questions to Ponder

In the Bible, God demonstrates His healing purposes in at least three categories: supernatural power, divine authority, and heavenly wisdom. Supernatural power relates to the use of healing graces, gifts, and anointing to accomplish healing. Divine authority releases healing by breaking curses, rebuking afflicting spirits, and exercising gifts of faith. Heavenly wisdom can take the form of natural cures, this is, the category that much of modern medicine functions under.

Notice how God used a "natural means" (heavenly wisdom-based healing) to cure Hezekiah in the book of Isaiah.

> *In those days Hezekiah became ill and was at the point of death. The prophet Isaiah son of Amoz went to him and said, "This is what the Lord says: 'Put your house in order, because you are going to die; you will not recover.'"*
>
> *Hezekiah turned his face to the wall and prayed to the Lord, "Remember, O Lord, how I have walked before you faithfully and with wholehearted devotion and have done what is good in your eyes." And Hezekiah wept bitterly.*
>
> *Then the word of the Lord came to Isaiah: "Go and tell Hezekiah, 'This is what the Lord, the God of your father David, says: I have heard your prayer and seen your tears; I will add fifteen years to your life... Isaiah had said, 'Prepare a poultice of figs and apply it to the boil, and he will recover.'"* (Isaiah 38:1-21)

1. Why would God say that Hezekiah would die if the cure was as simple as a "poultice of figs?"

_____

_____

_____

2. How is the power of sound and entrainment present in the healing of Hezekiah?

_____

_____

_____

3. Would you describe this healing as method or relationship?

_____

_____

_____

Further Study and Observation

Healing Experiment

Seek the Lord about how He might want to release healing in a friend or family member through a sound, a song, a prayer, or a declaration. Take time to get a firm sense of leading from the Lord. Step out in faith and ask your friend or family member if you can experiment with them to see if healing might be released through how you have been led. Practice gentleness, love, and kindness as you persevere in the leading you have from the Holy Spirit.

After administering the sound, song, prayer, or declaration, ask if there is any change in their condition. Take time to thank God for any changes in the person's condition and rejoice in their total healing. If there seems to be no difference, then thank the person for letting you experiment with them and confirm that you will continue to seek the Lord on their behalf. Go back to the Lord and see if there is any further leading or instruction. If not, then simply stand in faith and the assurance of obedience for what you have already done.

Check back with the person later and see if they are experiencing any changes. Encourage them that you are continuing to agree for their healing.

For Further Research

Professor Amnon Shiloah and **Singing the Ten Commandments**

Dr. Alfred A. Tomatis

Recommended Books on Healing

Healing the Sick: A Living Classic, by T. L. Osborn (1986)

Release the Power of Jesus, by Bill Johnson (2009)

God Can Use Little Ole Me, by Randy Clark (1998)

Authority From God, by Randy Clark (2006)

Christ the Healer, by F.F. Bosworth (2008)

God's Generals, by Roberts Liardon (2003)

Notes

_____

_____

_____

_____

_____

_____

_____

_____

_____

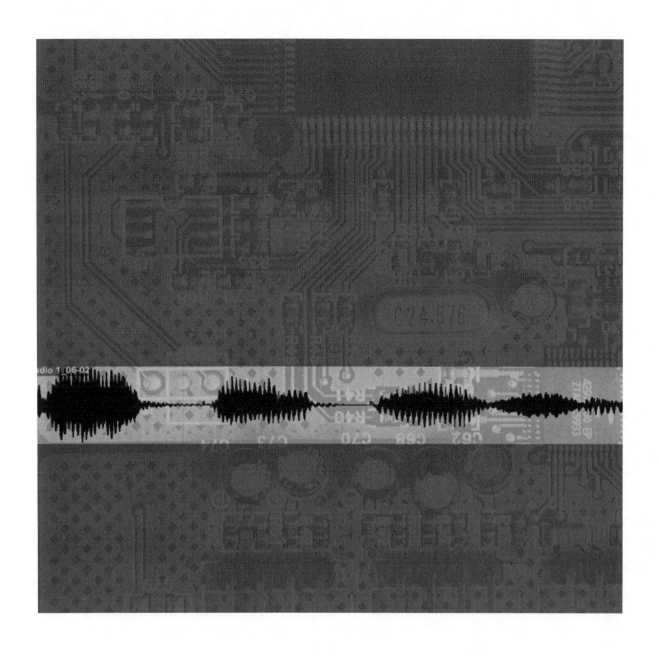

WHAT IF MUSIC
COULD STIMULATE HIGHER
BRAIN FUNCTION?

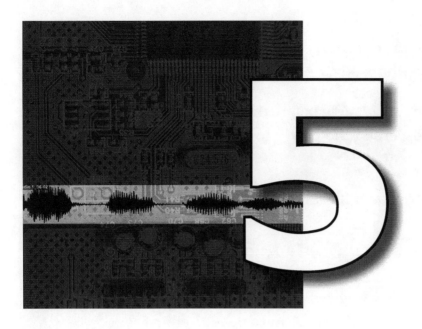

Synesthesia:
Music, Memory, and Creativity

We have observed the ability of sound and music to shape and form, to break and destroy, and to release healing. In this session, we will see sound's impact on the brain and our memories, as well as its power to stimulate our creativity.

1. Sound and music impact the entire _____ universe.

Music Shaping History

We see the powerful impact of music today. Consider the popularity and accessibility of analog and satellite radio, music television stations, TV competitions like "American Idol" and the "X Factor," digital music internet sites like iTunes, Napster, Rhapsody, and many others.

The following quotes show that long before the advent of modern technology, sound and music have possessed the power to shape history.

Plato (427-327 BC, Greek philosopher, student of Socrates, teacher of Aristotle)

> 2. "Give me the music of a generation and I will _____ the mind of that generation…. Music is a moral law, it gives soul to the universe, wings to the mind, flight to the imagination, and charm and gaiety to life and to everything."

> 3. Plato's philosophy was that one of the most powerful tools in the entire universe was _____ for affecting the mind, thought patterns, and creativity.

Blaise Pascal (1623-1662, French scientist, mathematician, and religious philosopher)

> 4. "The people who have the greatest influence in shaping the hearts and minds of any generation are not the folks who write the _____, but those who write the _____."

Ludwig van Beethoven (1770-1827, Virtuoso pianist, conductor, and composer)

> 5. "Music is a higher revelation than all wisdom and philosophy. Music is the _____ _____in which the spirit lives, thinks, and invents."

Albert Einstein (1879-1955, German-born theoretical physicist, 1921 Nobel Prize in Physics)

6. "If I were not a physicist, I would probably be a musician. I often think in music. I live my daydreams in music. I see my life in terms of music... Music was the driving force behind that intuition [theory of relativity]. My discovery was the result of _____ perception."[32]

7. Music may have the power to stimulate greater _____ and higher brain function.

8. You are eight times more likely to remember a _____ that is _____ than a sermon that is preached.

9. The word "music" comes from the word "muse" which literally means to _____ or "to ponder." So, the word "music" has in its very etymology that idea of the ability of music to control or influence thoughts.

Can Music Make Us Smarter?

Though the subject is still highly debated, many scientists and researchers believe that music and sound can stimulate higher brain function. These theories are consistent with the statements of Plato, Pascal, Beethoven, and Einstein. In 1995, researchers found higher SAT test scores among those students who were involved in music.

10. "As a whole, in 1995, SAT takers with coursework

---

[32] *The Saturday Evening Post*, 1926 October 26. An interview by George Sylvester Viereck "What Life Means to Einstein."

or experience in music performance scored 51 points higher on the _____ portion of the test, and 39 points higher on the _____ portion, as compared to students with no coursework or experience in the arts."[33]

The findings apply not only to adults; preschoolers have also shown an increased IQ when involved in music.

11. "Music lessons have been shown to improve children's performance in school. After eight months of keyboard lessons, a test group of preschoolers showed a 46% boost in their spatial IQ, which is _____ for higher brain functions such as complex math.[34]

12. We understand from these studies that music can actually stimulate higher _____ function and creativity.

Musical Memory

One theory for explaining higher test scores is that of musical memory. Songs have proven to improve memorization skills. Many adult Americans still internally recite the "ABC Song" when paging through a dictionary or phone book. It is difficult to separate the memory from the song.

13. We know that music impacts _____ because of how many of you grew up singing the ABC song.

---

[33] www.ufoc.org/Gail Crum, MENC informational services, 1-800-336-3768.
[34] Frances Rauscher, Ph.D. Gordon Shaw, Ph. D., University of California. Irvine National Coalition for Music Education.

Examples of musical memory songs include:

❖ The "ABC Song"

❖ Math Equation Songs

❖ Scripture Songs

❖ Nursery Rhymes

14. Musical memory can help _____ a greater understanding and retention.

MRI's of the brain have shown that music impacts eight unique centers of the brain. There are few activities that require more of the brain than playing music—auditory cortex, visual cortex, parietal lobe, motor cortex, sensory cortex, premotor area, frontal lobe, cerebellum are all stimulated musically.[35]

Songs of Remembrance

The link between music and memory may also have been used in the writing of biblical psalms. At least three psalms in the Bible carry the distinction "songs of remembrance."

❖ Psalm 38:1

❖ Psalm 70:1

❖ Psalm 77:6

These "songs of remembrance" are thought by some historians to carry a strong catchy melody that would cause the body of material to be easily recalled.

15. The purpose of psalms of remembrance is to help

---

[35]   Steven Fick and Elizabeth Shilts, "This is Your Brain on Music," *Canadian Geographic Magazine*, February 2008.

you remember a particular _____ or a
particular _____.

Synesthesia

Synesthesia may also be a factor impacting musical memory, higher brain function, and creativity. Synesthesia is a condition in which one sense (i.e., hearing) is simultaneously perceived as if by one or more additional senses, such as sight. Synesthesia can involve any of the senses but is most commonly found as seeing certain numbers or letters in color.

16. One example of synesthesia would be found in a person who, when hearing music, would involuntarily see _____.

Hertzian Scale of Visible Light

Though many people believe that sound and light exist on separate electromagnetic spectrums, (because sound as we know it cannot travel in a vacuum), there could be a direct link between their associated frequencies. If these vibrations are found on the same electromagnetic spectrum, then light would represent sound waves 41 octaves above middle C. We hear 10 octaves of sound and see only one octave of light, but light has a bandwidth many times greater than all 10 octaves of our hearing range. If we multiply the frequency of sound waves by the 41-octave equation, then a correlation could be made between musical notes and specific colors.

The middle C note vibrates at 523 times per second.
The middle G note vibrates at 783 times per second.
The middle F note vibrates at 689 times per second.

C	D	E	F	G	A	B
Yellow	Green	Blue	Indigo	Violet	Red	Orange

Conclusion

17. Understanding that there is a connection between sound, music, and the brain should make us take the power of our _____ much more seriously.

18. Music has the power to _____ the mindsets of generations.

19. We need to be much more careful with our words; we need to be much more _____ with the sound we are releasing.

The study of psychoacoustics helps us understand that how we say something affects what someone hears or how they interpret what is said.

20. Jesus as a person was the _____ of all of God's thoughts and ideas. He was the exact representation of the being and the nature of God. If you want to know anything about God, then you look at the person of Jesus Christ, because He personified the very will and purposes of God.

Music and sound have the power to shape the mindsets of generations, stimulate higher brain function, and prompt stronger memory and recall.

Remember that your life is sonifying something significant. Consider what dominant sound your life is making.

Life Application

Perhaps the link between music and memory is why new songs are so emphasized in Scripture.

> *Sing to the* Lord *a new song, sing to the* Lord*, all the earth.* (Psalm 96:1)

> *See, the former things have taken place, and* ***new things I declare; before they spring into being I announce them to you. Sing to the*** Lord ***a new song***, *his praise from the ends of the earth, you who go down to the sea, and all that is in it, you islands, and all who live in them.* (Isaiah 42:9-10, emphasis mine)

Is the command for everyone to sing a new song linked to its ability to impact the thoughts of a generation? Consider what God is saying: before something is released in the earth, He will announce it to His people so that they can sing a new song. To understand that this is inclusive of everyone, He names various geographical locations in the next several verses. The new song is for those from the ends of the earth, the islands, the deserts, the towns and settlements, and for those who live on the mountaintops. These verses labor to show each individual's responsibility to carry the new song of God.

A song—or music—carries the power to change and often radically shape mindsets.

Questions for Group Discussion

1. In light of this lesson, do you believe that your musical choices shape your thinking? How so, or why not?

_____

_____

_____

2. What music most stimulates your own creativity?

_____

_____

_____

3. How do you use music to set a mood, express a mood, or create an atmosphere?

_____

_____

_____

4. What is the believer's responsibility for carrying the "new song"? How does this manifest itself in your life?

_____

_____

_____

Questions to Ponder

1. What songs involuntarily stir up memories for you?

_____

_____

_____

2. In what ways have you ever used music as a memorization tool?

_____

_____

_____

3. How might you intentionally apply music for increased memory function or to stimulate creativity?

_____

_____

_____

4. How do your current music choices positively or negatively affect your thinking, atmosphere, creativity, or memories?

_____

_____

_____

Further Study and Observation

Musical Synesthesia Experiment

Close your eyes while having someone play a single note on a musical instrument. Write down the color you saw when that note was being played. You can perform this several times with different notes. Now compare the colors you saw to the Hertzian scale of visible light to discover whether you were seeing the actual color of the note.

C	D	E	F	G	A	B
Yellow	Green	Blue	Indigo	Violet	Red	Orange

Further Research

Synesthesia: Take the tests at **www.synesthete.org**

Musical Biofeedback

Mozart Effect

Musical Memory

Heart Memory

Recommended Resources on the Mind

The Art of Thinking Brilliantly teaching series by Graham Cooke

The Supernatural Power of a Transformed Mind by Bill Johnson, Destiny Image (2005)

Notes

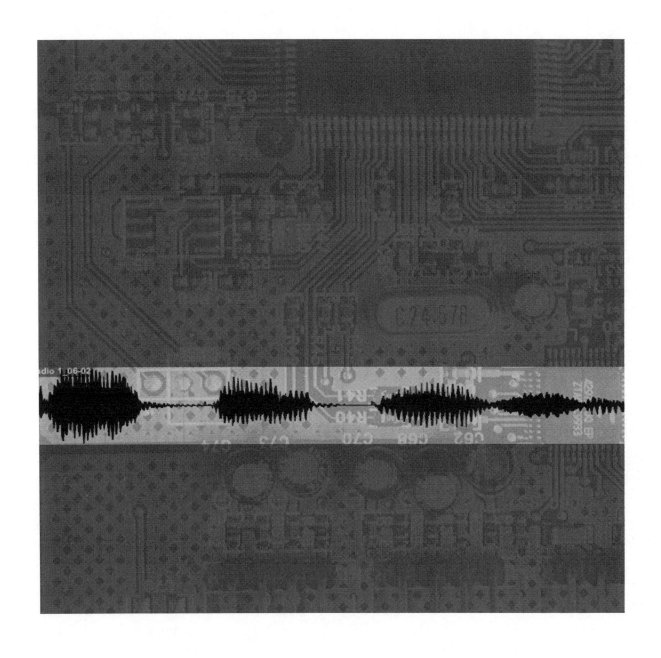

WHAT IF SOUNDS
COULD OPEN AND CLOSE SPIRITUAL
PORTALS?

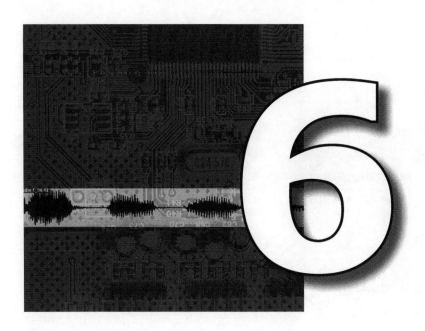

Spiritual Entrainment:
Sounds of Heaven and Earth

In this lesson you will discover how vibrations, frequency, resonance and entrainment impact the spiritual world. The former lessons have led to this grand finale of encountering greater and deeper realms of the Spirit through all that we have studied and learned. Paul prayed that the churches would be given a spirit of revelation and understanding for a deeper God encounter. In the same spirit, I pray that God would increase your ability to connect all of our prior information to its greater application in a powerful climax of the spiritual dimension.

1. Sound and music not only impact the physical universe, they also _____ us with spiritual realms and spiritual realities.

2. Sound or music can _____ spiritual encounters.

The double-portion prophet Elisha was asked by a king to prophesy concerning the future of the nation. Elisha responded by asking them to first bring him a harpist. It was while the harpist played that the Spirit of the Lord came upon Elisha, enabling him to connect with the word of the Lord.

Elisha said..."But now bring me a harpist." While the harpist was playing, the hand of the LORD came upon Elisha and he said....(2 Kings 3:14-16)

3. Elisha understood that an anointed musician had the potential to open up a _____ or a gateway for an encounter with God.

Elisha's example was not an isolated incident in Scripture. Saul, son of Kish, was also impacted prophetically by a group of musical prophets.

After that you will go to Gibeah of God, where there is a Philistine outpost. As you approach the town, you will meet a procession of prophets coming down from the high place with lyres, tambourines, flutes and harps being played before them, and they will be prophesying. The Spirit of the LORD will come upon you in power, and you will prophesy with them; and you will be changed into a different person. Once these signs are fulfilled, do whatever your hand finds to do, for God is with you. (1 Samuel 10:5-7)

Notice the three-fold result of coming into the atmosphere of these musical prophets:

❖ The Spirit of the Lord came upon him in power—he encounters God.

❖ He prophesied—the spirit of prophecy comes upon him.

❖ His heart was changed into a different person—he was transformed.

These guys who prophesied on their instruments were creating an atmosphere into which other people could enter to encounter the same anointing that was upon the prophets' lives.

    4. The prophets were actually creating a habitation of God that became an _____ to others.

    5. The goal for those of us who want to be prophetic musicians is not just to be able to deliver a prophetic song, but to carry a prophetic _____.

Conversion through an Atmosphere

I encountered a modern-day version of a man's heart being changed into another person through a prophetic musical encounter in India. While teaching at a worship school in Thailand, I met Chris from Assam, a restricted entry state in the northeast of India. Chris came from a strict Hindu family that was known to persecute Christians. When I asked Chris how he came to know the Lord, he told me that it was in a tent where people were worshiping.

Chris entered the tent not knowing what the people were actually doing. He was merely attracted by the atmosphere they were creating.

"As I stood there enjoying the sound," Chris explained to me, "someone tapped me on the shoulder and asked, 'Would you like to know what they are doing?'"

"Yes...I would," Chris responded.

The voice answered, "They are worshiping Me."

At this point in the story, I interrupted Chris, "What do you mean? Who was it?" I asked.

Chris looked at me with surprise and said in a matter-of-fact tone, "It was Jesus."

Chris continued his story. "Then He asked me if I would like to know Him the way these people did, and I answered, 'Yes!'"

"Wait a minute!" I interrupted again, "You mean, Jesus led you to...Jesus? That's amazing!"

Ever since that day, Chris has been a worship leader and preacher. His heart had been changed into another man in an atmosphere of worship.

> 6. A good evangelistic plan would be: "Get into _____ with Heaven, begin to praise God until He inhabits it, and then just invite people into that atmosphere.

Non-believers, or people with a non-God agenda, have been impacted by similar encounters in various biblical accounts. One of my favorites appears in First Samuel chapter 19.

> *Word came to Saul: "David is in Naioth at Ramah;" so he sent men to capture him. But when they saw a group of prophets prophesying, with Samuel standing there as their leader, the Spirit of God came upon Saul's men and they also prophesied. Saul was told about it, and he sent more men, and they prophesied too. Saul sent men a third time, and they also prophesied. Finally, he himself left for Ramah...But the Spirit of God came even upon him, and he walked along prophesying until he came to Naioth. He stripped off his robes and also prophesied in Samuel's presence. He lay that way all that day and night. This is why people say, "Is Saul also among the prophets?"* (1 Samuel 19:19-24)

Remember that the Spirit of the Lord did not come on many people during this period of biblical history. So, for these military men of Saul's to encounter the presence of the Lord—to have the spirit of prophecy come upon them so powerfully—certainly would have been a life-changing experience. Notice that the armies of men described in this account were not seeking God nor did they have a godly agenda, but were, nevertheless, impacted in the atmosphere created by this prophetic company.

Likewise, your worship, prayers, and prophetic proclamations can actually become an atmospheric anointing that others can enter in to. The breakthrough you create has the potential of becoming a territorial "divine radiation zone" of the presence and power of God.

7. What are we looking for? We are looking for an entrainment with Heaven that becomes an atmosphere of _____ that becomes a _____ spirit.

8. Prophesying is _____ what God is _____.

9. The goal of the power of sound is to _____ you with the one who spoke you into existence.

10. We just want to make the sound that God is making in this moment and _____ it in the earth so that it can have its purpose, so that our breakthrough becomes an increasingly enlarging atmosphere that others can enjoy until the Kingdom of God is manifest on Earth as it is in Heaven.

11. Sound can also _____ spiritual encounters.

Sounds and music from the earth can open up spiritual encounters, but sounds from heaven can also announce the spiritual realm in the earth. There are dozens of examples in Scripture of a sound occurring just before something wonderful or glorious happens in a spiritual dimension. It would appear that heavenly sounds often preclude spiritual events released in Heaven and Earth. Here are just a few examples:

Then the man and his wife **heard the sound of the LORD God as he was walking** *in the garden in the cool of the day....*(Genesis 3:8, emphasis mine)

On the morning of the third day there was thunder and lightning, with a thick cloud over the mountain, and **a very loud trumpet blast**. *Everyone in the camp trembled. Then Moses led the people out of the camp to meet with God, and they stood at the foot of the mountain. Mount Sinai was covered with smoke, because the LORD descended on it in fire. The smoke billowed up from it like smoke from a furnace, the whole mountain trembled violently, and* **the sound of the trumpet grew louder and louder. Then Moses spoke and the voice of God answered him**. (Exodus 19:16-19, emphasis mine)

12. One of the things I have learned about interacting with heavenly sights, heavenly sounds, and heavenly encounters is that the more you _____ God in them, and turn aside to encounter them, the louder, the stronger, and the clearer they get.

13. The closer they got—the more they pressed towards God to hear His voice—the _____ the sounds of Heaven became.

In a flash, in the twinkling of an eye, at the last trumpet. **For the trumpet will sound**, *the dead will be raised imperishable, and we will be changed.* (1 Corinthians 15:52, emphasis mine)

> *Then the seven angels who had the seven trumpets **prepared to sound them**.* (Revelation 8:6, emphasis mine)

Heaven and Earth Can Interact in Sound

The essence of prayer, worship, and prophesy can be described as the interaction between sounds of Earth and the power of Heaven. Scripture often describes times of interchange between the sounds of Heaven and Earth.

> *When the day of Pentecost came, they were all together in one place. **Suddenly a sound like the blowing of a violent wind** came from heaven and filled the whole house where they were sitting. They saw what seemed to be tongues of fire that separated and came to rest on each of them. All of them were filled with the Holy Spirit and **began to speak in other tongues** as the Spirit enabled them. Now there were staying in Jerusalem God-fearing Jews from every nation under heaven. When they heard this sound, a crowd came together in bewilderment, because each one heard them speaking in his own language.* (Acts 2:1-6, emphasis mine)

> 14. The sound that drew the people was a sound that they made in _____ to the sound they heard from Heaven.

Notice that it was not the sound of a mighty, rushing wind that drew the crowd of thousands to salvation, but rather, it was the sound that men and women were making in response to Heaven's outpouring. At this moment, the voice that was heard was "from every nation under Heaven" making a God-sound all together. This day of Pentecost stands as a turning point in history when representatives from the church began responding to the outpouring of Heaven in the language and sound of every nation, tongue, and tribe on Earth. Whenever Heaven and Earth make the same sound, powerful things happen. Psalm 67 is another example of this principle.

May the peoples praise you, O God; may all the people praise you. **Then the land will yield its harvest**, *and God, our* **God, will bless us**. *God will bless us, and* **all the ends of the earth will fear Him**. (Psalm 67:5-7, emphasis mine)

15. God is calling for a sound from the earth that
_____ the sound from Heaven.

When all the people praise God, there is a three-fold response.

16. First the _____ responds
to the praises of the people and yields its harvest.

This is both symbolic and actual. Men's prayers, prophetic proclamations, and praise songs can literally affect the ecology and economy of a nation. (Example: Elijah's prayer to withhold rain from the earth certainly affected his nation for three and a half years! See James 5:17.)

17. The second effect of the praises of all people is that
_____ responds with blessings.

Our prayers, proclamations, and praises invite God to release His best purposes in the earth.

18. Finally, the praises of people impact the
_____ of the earth.

In Psalm 67, we can see the transformational power of sound in the earth. Remember the earth still responds to the sound of the voice that created it.

Humans are impacted by sound on every level of their consciousness, and God has chosen to respond with blessings to the praises of mankind.

Spiritual Entrainment

Physical entrainment is the tendency of two oscillating bodies of the same frequency to resonate together. There is also a principle of spiritual entrainment that unlocks the impossible realm. When we are in harmony or unity with the word and will of God, then nothing is impossible.

> *Again, I tell you that if two of you on earth agree about anything you ask for, it will be done for you by my Father in heaven. For where two or three come together in my name, there am I with them.* (Matthew 18:19)

"Agree" is the Greek word *sumphoneo*[36] which means "to sound together, of sounds and of musical instruments; to be in accord, to harmonize." When two or three people harmonize or resonate together in a spiritual entrainment, then God is in the midst of them, and whatever they ask will be done. Throughout Scripture, whenever people came into this level of agreement (entrainment), it resulted in a revival or a riot, depending on whether they were tuned to God's voice or not.

> *If you remain in me and my words remain in you, ask whatever you wish, and it will be given you.* (John 15:7)

Let me paraphrase this verse in the terminology of our study: if you resonate with God and His word is resonating in you, then all of Heaven and Earth will respond to the sounds you release.

Whenever a person, place, or thing is resonating on Heaven's frequency, then something powerful and wonderful occurs. The greatest frequency in the universe, the dominant of all frequencies, is the voice of the Lord. You can choose to resonate on that frequency!

---

[36] *Thayer's Greek Lexicon*, 04856.

Conclusion

All things in the universe—visible and invisible—still respond to the voice that created them. When we resonate with Heaven, anything is possible!

Life Application

A number of years ago the National Science Foundation estimated that our brains produce as many as 12,000 to 50,000 thoughts per day depending on how "deep" a thinker you are. Other estimates run as high as 60,000 thoughts per day! For the average person, 80% of thoughts are negative. These thoughts have often been called "self-talk."[37]

Now that you understand the power of entrainment, what implications do you think this amount of negative self-talk might have for your mental, physical, emotional, and spiritual health?

_____

_____

What can I do about negative self-talk?

1. Identify when you are thinking negatively.
2. Challenge the thought, and don't give it a right to be there.
3. Replace your negative thought with a God-thought.
4. Repeat God thoughts several times a day until they become your thinking pattern.

Write down at least 12 positive, truthful statements in the present tense. Practice displacing your negative self talk by focusing on these positive truths.

---

[37] Some information adapted from http://www.sound-mind.org/positive-self-talk.html

Try writing each of your sentences in the first person.

"I am..."

_____

_____

_____

"I no longer...instead I..."

_____

_____

_____

"I do..."

_____

_____

_____

"I can..."

_____

_____

_____

Not all your statements have to be done this way. These are simply examples for you to practice speaking truthful statements about yourself.

Notes

Questions for Group Discussion

1. Whose voice do you feel you are most resonating with at this time in your life (i.e., self, others, God, the enemy)?

_____

_____

_____

2. What sound is that voice making?

_____

_____

_____

3. How are you coming into entrainment with the voice of God?

_____

_____

_____

4. What do you feel God is speaking in you, to you, and through you right now?

_____

_____

_____

Questions to Ponder

1. Often this teaching on *God Vibrations: The Power of Sound* stimulates the question: "How can I interact more with the sound of Heaven?" What are your thoughts for increasing your own entrainment with Heaven?

_____

_____

_____

2. How will this chapter impact your practice of prayer, worship, and prophetic declarations?

_____

_____

_____

Further Study and Observation

Spiritual Sensitivity Experiment

Next time you are in a worship service or corporate prayer meeting, experiment with your own spiritual sensitivities. Watch for sights, sounds, tastes, smells, or tactile sensations that might trigger a deeper spiritual awareness or encounter. If a sensation begins, check for a natural cause; if none is found, acknowledge the Lord is at work.

Also watch for changes in the atmosphere. Is there an increased volume or increased stillness in certain moments? Dialogue with the Holy Spirit. Acknowledge that He is at work and ask Him what He is doing in those moments.

By experimenting with your spiritual sensitivities you can "train yourself to be godly"[38] and often increase the supernatural activity in your life.

Recommended Books

For more reading on increasing your spiritual sensitivities, I recommend the following books:

- ❖ *The School of the Seers: A Practical Guide*, by Jonathan Welton, Destiny Image, 2009.

- ❖ *Developing a Supernatural Lifestyle*, by Kris Vallotton, Destiny Image, 2007.

- ❖ *Open My Eyes, Lord: A Practical Guide to Angelic Visitations and Heavenly Experiences*, by Gary Oates, Open Heaven Publications, 2005.

- ❖ *Experiencing the Heavenly Realms*, by Judy Franklin and Beni Johnson, Destiny Image, 2011.

---

[38] 1 Timothy 4:7-8.

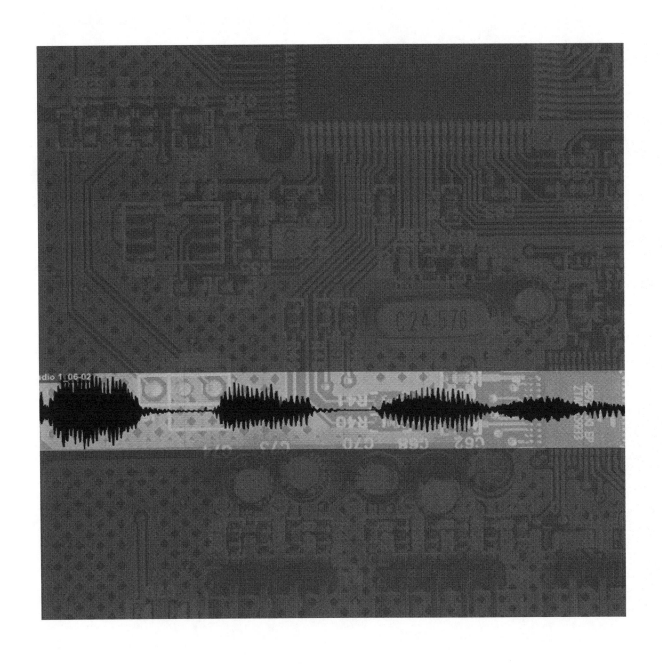

WHAT SHOULD BE DONE WITH WHAT
WE HAVE LEARNED?

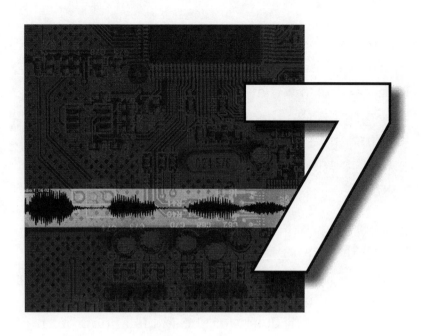

Sonic Impact

I f you are the kind of person who reads book introductions, you know that my personal introductory story left us on a tropical hilltop in the Fiji Islands with me in the midst of an epiphany regarding the power of sound. The research and exploration in *God Vibrations Study Guide* accounts for the seven years of study following that God encounter. While I think that the journey into the power of sound is in itself a fascinating and worthwhile exploration, I am just pragmatic enough to ask, "What should be done with what we have learned? What is the personal sonic impact of this knowledge of the power of sound?" So, in conclusion, I would like to share just a bit more of my personal journey and how I have responded to these new revelations.

Since my initial revelations happened during a worship service, I knew that my primary mission relating to the power of sound involved worship. In response to this realization, my wife and I started a non-profit organization called Sounds of the Nations whose mission is to equip and empower indigenous people to write and record authentic, ethnic expressions of worship in every tribe, nation, and tongue. It seemed to me that if the very first manifestation of the outpouring of the Holy Spirit on the Day of Pentecost (Acts 2) was that the gathered people were hearing the praises of God in their own language and responding by praising God in their own ethnic styles, then sound and language must be really important.

I believe in testing ideas and leadings of the Holy Spirit; but as an old African proverb says, "No one tests the depths of a river with both feet." Through prayer, counsel, and contemplation, it seemed reasonable to return to the country of Fiji where I first felt the call in order to test the sonic impact of my new revelations. So I purchased an airline ticket for the Fiji Islands from my home in Northern California and made arrangements to meet with about one hundred worship leaders from various churches from the Islands. The word God had spoken to my heart loomed large and intimidating:

> *You will change the sound of worship in nations. You are destined for the rise and fall of nations.* (See Luke 2:34, originally in reference to the life and mission of Jesus.)

By the time I had purchased my ticket and made my accommodations and meeting arrangements, I only had a few hundred dollars left to my name. I held the remaining money before the Lord and asked sincerely, "How am I supposed to change nations with only this?" There was no immediate answer.

The next day, however, I was leafing through a musical instrument catalogue and saw an advertisement for sets of guitar strings priced at only one dollar and fifty cents each. In America, these would usually cost between six and sixteen dollars each. The little light in my head went on as I thought, *It is not much, but I could give every person who attends my first worship conference in Fiji a free set of guitar strings.*

I sent off for the strings one week before my departure.

That Friday evening, I was speaking at a church in Sacramento, California, and a man came up to me at the close of the service. Almost trembling, he said, "I feel like the Lord told me to give you my guitar and it has something to do with music and missions. Does that make any sense to you?"

I replied, "It sure does. I know exactly what that means." I opened the lid of the guitar case and gazed upon an Eric Clapton Signature Model 000-28 Martin acoustic guitar valued from $3000-$5000. The generosity of this gift overwhelmed me.

Then the thought of Fijian humidity hit me. I asked him, "My upcoming mission is in Fiji. I know the extreme humid weather there would destroy this guitar. What would be your preference with this guitar—give it away or sell it?"

The man replied, "Do whatever you want with it, but use it for music and missions."

I posted the guitar on Craigslist for a quick turnaround and sold it within 24 hours. That Saturday, I used the money to purchase microphones, cables, and cords that would travel easily in a suitcase and be suitable for the climate of Fiji.

The Sunday morning before my Tuesday departure, I attended The Mission Church, my home congregation in Northern California. My friend, Greg, excitedly greeted me, celebrating that he had just purchased a new guitar. In guitar-player culture, purchasing a new guitar is the equivalent of having a baby. We oohed and aahed over his baby for a while, and then Greg said, "I don't know what I am going to do with my old guitar though. Hey! Aren't you going to Fiji this week?"

"Yes, I am," I replied. Since I had not told anyone about what I was really going to be doing in Fiji, I was surprised by what I thought he was implying.

"Why don't you take it and see if anyone there needs it?"

"What a generous offer...thank you so much," I answered. Bending down, I opened the guitar case and discovered a shallow bowl Ovation Custom Balladeer with a sunburst finish. The fiberglass backing on this guitar made it a perfect match for Fijian humidity. I was amazed at this provision.

As I was leaving church that morning carrying the Ovation guitar in one hand, and my Bible in the other, another couple stopped me.

"We felt like we were supposed to buy a guitar to send with you to Fiji," they said to me, pressing several hundred dollars into my hand. "We do not know anything about the Fijians, so we just decided to give you a money gift to purchase what you need."

Wow! Within three days I had been given three guitars, and I had not told anyone what I was going to be doing in Fiji.

I took the cash to a local guitar store and tried out about twenty different guitars in the price range of what had been gifted to me for the Fiji trip. The best of the lot was a cobalt blue Fender Stratocaster in a nylon gig bag. My strings also arrived in the mail that day. Reflecting back in awe, I realized that only one week previous, I held my few hundred dollars before the Lord inquiring about what significance could be made with such little money. Now I was leaving for Fiji with 144 sets of guitar strings, thousands of dollars of microphones, cables, and cords, an Ovation Custom Balladeer acoustic guitar worth between six to eight hundred dollars, and a brand new cobalt blue Fender Stratocaster. I love it when you find God's fingerprints all over what you are doing!

As I settled in to Fiji and we started the first day of meetings, I stood before our group of worship leaders and greeted them. "Before I start, I would like to give you a little thank you gift for coming. I would like to give each of you a set of guitar strings."

The response was overwhelming. A local missionary later informed me that guitar strings on this island could cost up to three months' wages. My "little" gift to each worship leader was considered very generous.

At the close of the meeting, a man came up to me with tears in his eyes. He was holding a guitar in his hand with only three strings left on it. The tuning pegs were mostly broken off and copper coins and had been welded in their place. "You don't understand," he said choking back tears, "I come from a small island of about four hundred people. This is the only instrument on the island." I was humbled by this information. He continued, "When you gave me these guitar strings, you changed the sound of worship on my island."

"What did you say?" I almost shouted in amazement.

He repeated the words, "You changed the sound of worship on my island."

Now I was the one in tears. His words were an exact fulfillment of what God had spoken to me about changing the sound of worship in nations, but I never imagined it could be done for one dollar and fifty cents worth of guitar strings. God was speaking, confirming a greater mission and His divine ability to do beyond what we ask, think, or even imagine.

The next day, I returned to the Bible college where I first had the epiphany. At the college, I met a young man who was doing an amazing outreach among Muslims. He was literally seeing hundreds finding the joy of new life in relationship with Jesus Christ. I asked if he had any prayer requests, and he responded that he was praying for a guitar. I believe in being specific in prayer, so I asked him what kind of guitar he was praying for. "For two years I have had a picture on the wall of the guitar I am praying for—an Ovation Custom Balladeer," he answered.

"I can't pray for that," I responded.

He looked a little surprised and questioned, "Am I asking for too much?"

"No," I replied. "I can't pray for it because your answer is out in the jeep. Go and get it!" The guitar Greg had given me was the exact model and color this young Fijian evangelist had spent two years praying for.

In another meeting, a man at the back of the auditorium caught my eye. I felt like this man was to be the recipient of the thousands of dollars of microphones, cables, and cords I had brought. "Is that man a pastor?" I inquired.

"Yes," my missionary friend responded.

"Would it be culturally appropriate to give him some microphones and cables?" I asked.

My friend looked shocked, "It would be amazing!"

We called the man forward after the meeting and gave him the equipment. He did not speak much English, but he pulled out a microphone and sang tear-filled praises to God for more than thirty minutes. The missionary friend gave me the back story. Two or three years previous, a generous group from New Zealand had given the man a sound system for his church. The pastor and congregation were very thankful but could never afford the microphones, cables, and cords to make it work. Here I had called him out of a large group, with no prior knowledge of this situation, and handed him the very thing they needed to make their sound of worship.

As my trip came to a close, I still had the cobalt blue Fender Stratocaster. When I asked the Lord what I should do with it, I was really surprised by the answer. I felt a strong impression to give it to the teenage son of the missionary.

"Does your son play guitar?" I asked my friend.

"Yes..." the missionary answered in more of a question than an answer.

"Well, I feel like I am supposed to give him a guitar. Would that be okay?"

Now the missionary was crying, "That would be amazing!"

I called in the young man and told him that I felt God wanted him to have this guitar. He opened the case and started shouting, "This is the one! This is the one!" Now he and his dad were embracing. The young man thanked me and ran off with the guitar. His dad told me the story. His son had wanted to start playing guitar but there were very few available in the islands at that time. They had found one guitar that a church was willing to sell. The guitar was a beat up old Fender Stratocaster copy and it was—you guessed it!—cobalt blue. The son had worked for months to raise the money to purchase the guitar. But, when he went to buy it, the church had changed its mind and sold it to someone else. The young man was crushed. Disappointment and disillusionment affected his relationship with God as well as the churches of Fiji. The guitar I gave him on this day was the same model, make, and color but was an original in brand new condition, not a copy.

I returned from Fiji overwhelmed at God's goodness and the specific leading of the Holy Spirit. All of these miraculous testimonies served as confirmation that God truly had a mission for me in releasing an indigenous sound of worship in the islands.

Today, our organization is active in at least twenty-four nations and language groups. Our ten-year goal is to reach the 389 language groups that represent 98% of the world's population.

Apply the Power of Sound

The implications of what I learned through this study have led me to several conclusions for how to apply the power of sound to my personal calling.

Everything Vibrates

The first lesson taught me that since sound was vital to the creation and existence of all things, we should take our songs and particular sounds and instruments more seriously. What we say, how we say it, how we sing it, and how it sounds are all significant to understanding the atmospheres we create and the reality that we release.

Every Vibration Makes a Sound

The second lesson unveiled the importance of every sound. Every instrument and every voice has a distinct sound. Every sound has a distinct impact. As I listen to ethnic instruments and vocal patterns and intervals, I find myself hunting for the distinctions of what that sound is creating or releasing. I have crossed the hurdle of personal preference and style to a deep honor and value for every sound, style, and instrument. I have found that instruments from a specific geographic region may have the greatest impact on the environment of that region. It could be that the materials from the land they are made of—clay, metals, woods, and organic materials—have the potential to literally cause that land to align with Heaven and rejoice in the Lord.

The Breaker Power of Sound

This shows me a new way to do spiritual warfare over a geographical region. I began to question how the Church had done missions in the past. When we go into a culture and tell them their sound is evil or "of the devil," then the only ones making the sound of that people and that land—what we would consider in this study to be the dominant frequency of that people group and geographical area—are those who are not aligning with the sound of Heaven. Therefore, it could be possible that this style of ministry is giving more power to the enemies of darkness and less power to the Church. Beyond the issue of cultural contextualization for evangelism are the bigger implications of how Heaven, Earth, and spiritual forces respond to particular sounds. We have seen significant breakthroughs in spiritual freedom through lifting up praises using the original ethnic sounds of a particular region.

The Healing Power of Sound

I have seen the healing power of sound countless times in our meetings and through our global partners around the world. I have witnessed people healed from deafness, forms of blindness, bone diseases, curvature of the spine, and even autism, through sounds, songs, and declarations.

Music, Memory, and Creativity

This lesson has drastically affected our song writing and song choices. Understanding the impact of our lyrics on the mind, memory, and physical reality has made it impossible to sing some of the things we used to sing. At the same time, our teams around the world are really listening for what God is saying and doing in the Church in this season and trying to capture those things in new songs that shape how generations will think.

The Sounds of Heaven and Earth

Our final lesson is, for me, an unending journey into the fullness God wants to express to all of His children. Prayers, praises, and proclamations are portals for spiritual encounters with a loving and willing God. We have seen scores of people born again during a worship service. We have also seen hundreds break off the amulets and cords given to them by witch doctors and lay them on the stage with no preaching or prompting. The authentic sounds they lifted up create an atmosphere of connection with God, and their response was repentance from evil. Furthermore, I have seen the power of praises and prayers transform the atmosphere in my own home with my wife and children.

The testimonies and lessons I have shared are only the humble beginnings of a much greater journey into the power of sound. Though you may not have the call to redeem ethnic sounds in nations around the world, the power of sound is as much a part of your journey as it is mine.

Every day your words—and how you say them—are affecting multiple realities and dimensions around you. I have shared with you in this conclusion the next chapter of my journey, but now it is time for you to explore the next chapter of yours. You have seen things in the videos and read things in this manual that I believe will forever change you—how you think, how you speak, how you listen, even what you believe. Yet it is your response to these truths that will turn information and inspiration into transformation. It is applying and doing the truth through partnership and dialogue with the Holy Spirit that makes the sonic impact of these lessons more than an interesting study.

My prayer for you is that this conclusion would not be "the end," but rather, that it would be the beginning of your journey.

Appendix

Answers to the Fill-in-the-Blanks

Lesson One

1. God

2. anything / creator

3. could not

4. invisible

5. created being

6. pleasure

7. turn them

8. create

9. something / nothing

10. vibration

11. shape

12. shapes

13. vibrations

14. shape / structure

15. physical matter

16. God

17. sound

18. vibrates / motion

19. speed

Lesson Two

1. re-sound

2. resonating

3. symphony

4. convey / data

5. warning song

6. salvation

7. manifest

8. 234 million

9. human

10. compare

11. mutations

12. tunes

13. resonance

14. song / songs

Lesson Three

1. together
2. unstable
3. striking
4. one another
5. obedience
6. voice
7. break
8. prison
9. destroy
10. sonic weapon
11. aligning
12. agreeing

Lesson Four

1. healing
2. human voice
3. imporve / maintain
4. emotional
5. physical
6. spiritual
7. impact / transform
8. harmony
9. resonance

10. tune
11. body / organs
12. bones
13. air
14. resonate
15. agreement
16. healing
17. truth

Lesson Five

1. physical
2. change
3. music
4. laws / songs
5. electric soil
6. musical
7. creativity
8. song / sung
9. think
10. verbal / math
11. crucial
12. brain
13. memory
14. presevere
15. idea /story

16. color

17. songs

18. shape

19. sensitive

20. sonification

Lesson Six

1. connect

2. invite

3. portal

4. invitation

5. atmosphere

6. agreement

7. breakthrough / breakthrough

8. saying / saying

9. reconnect

10. release

11. announce

12. acknowledge

13. louder

14. response

15. matches

16. earth

17. God

18. people

About the Author

Dan McCollam travels internationally as a prophetic speaker and trainer. He strategizes with churches and individuals to create prophetic cultures in which everyone can hear God, activate and mobilize their prophetic words, and express their own unique prophetic diversity.

Dan has developed many resources that offer a fresh perspective on the prophetic, supernatural Kingdom life, biblical character and spiritual gifting. He is well-known as a great friend of the Holy Spirit and one who carries and imparts wisdom, revelation, and breakthrough.

Dan serves on the teaching faculty of Bethel School of the Prophets and Bethel School of Worship in Redding, California. He is part of the Global Legacy apostolic team that oversees a growing number of churches in partnership for revival. He serves on the core leadership team at his home church, Mission Church, in Vacaville, California, with his wife Regina, and is a director of the Deeper School of Supernatural Life also in Vacaville.

Sounds of the Nations and iWar

After serving as a worship leader for 20 years and releasing Kingdom worshipers locally, regionally, and globally on countless mission trips to nations around the world, Dan became troubled over the westernization of worship in the majority of churches in which he ministered. Indigenous sounds had often been labeled sinful by church leadership. Since the sounds of every tribe and nation are heard in Heaven, becoming an agent in restoring the stolen authentic expressions of worship became a driving passion for Dan, and Sounds of the Nations was born.

As international director of Sounds of the Nations and the Institute for Worship Arts Resources (iWar), Dan trains indigenous peoples to write and record worship songs using their own ethnic sounds, styles, languages, and instruments.

The Worship Writer's Guide
Dan McCollam

Fourteen lyrical and melodic tools for crafting excellent praise and worship songs.

Creativity is not just inspiration; it also has its deep roots in wisdom, knowledge, and understanding. *The Worship Writer's Guide* is designed to give you the song crafting tools that are based on the timeless principles of great songwriting.

Available for sale at iBethel.org/store, store.iMissionChurch.com and Amazon.com

Book (85 pages): $10   Kindle Version available

Visit iBethel.org/store or
store.iMissionChurch.com
online
and search for "Dan McCollam" or
"Sounds of the Nations".

Original worship music from Sounds of the
Nations is also available on iTunes.

Understanding Your Metron
Dan McCollam

Explore the demographic and geographic spheres of influence where your prophetic gift has the greatest authority, influence and favor.

Audio CD : $10   MP3 Download : $4

Encouragement
Dan McCollam

Many people feel that correction or judgment is a higher level of prophetic operation. This message reveals the true expressions of prophetic maturity. Encouragement is the mother tongue of the Holy Spirit.

Audio CD (1) : $10   MP3 Download: $4

Anachronistic Living:
Pulling Future Prophetic Promises into Present Reality
Dan McCollam

In this message from The Prophetic Series, you will discover the principles of how to live powerfully and practically in the present while possessing a prophetic vision for a more desirable future.

Audio CD (1) : $10   MP3 Download: $4

Prophetic Culture and Identity

Dan McCollam

Prophetic Culture and identity is a two-part series. In this series, you will be taken on a journey to discover the ingredients for creating prophetic culture. Then learn the craft of defining yourself by how Heaven sees you.

Audio CD (1) : $10   MP3 Download: $4

Living on the Right Side of the Cross
EXTENDED VERSION
Dan McCollam

The six-session extended version of the popular original release, Living on the Right Side of the Cross, is now available.

Session One: The Wrong Side
Recognize the symptoms of not fully understanding the benefits of the cross.

Session Two: Getting on the Right Side
Renew your mind with four power positions vital to living on the right side of the cross.

Session Three: Dealing with Sin and Temptation
Unpack practical and theological principles reinforcing your victory over sin.

Session Four: The Ascended Lifestyle
Grasp the glories of the present tense realities of the resurrection.

Session Five: Accessing the Ascended Lifestyle
Discover two keys to accessing the benefits of living on the right side of the cross.

Session Six: New Creation Realities
Say goodbye to the "Adam's Family" and hello to your inheritance in the "last Adam," Jesus Christ.

Audio CDs (3) : $25   MP3 Download: $15

Sounds of the Nations
Volumes 1, 2 and 3

A musical sampling of "every tribe and tongue" that are to be represented in heaven.

CD or Digital Download
Volume One
Featuring songs from India, Romania, and the Philippines.

Volume Two
A musical journey through India, South Africa, Thailand, Dominican Republic, and Fiji.

Volume Three
Experience the praises of Israel, Australia and South Africa.

Available at iTunes or store.iMissionChurch.com

We Love You Baba
Sounds of the Nations Africa

The sound of African orphans in worship. The ethnic rhythms, sounds, and joyful praises of African orphans.

CD or Digital Download

Available at iTunes or store.iMissionChurch.com

Made in the USA
Columbia, SC
21 February 2024